MESILA
Providing the Path to Financial Stability

Mesila's Financial Literacy Mini-Course

Based on Mesila's Financial Literacy Program

Student Resources

MESILA
Providing The Path to Financial Stability

Mesila's Financial Literacy Mini-Course

Student Resources

ISBN 978-1-941902-32-5

Authored by:
Malky Heimowitz
and Batya Weinberg

Questions or comments may be sent to:

Mesila
P.O.B. 57116
Jerusalem 9157002, Israel
Tel: +972.2.500.0475
Fax: +972.2.500.0478
info@mesila.org
www.mesila.org
Reg. Amuta No. 580361236
Tax ID No. 11-3597720

Please note:

This material is intended for use exclusively in the context of a Mesila-authorized course. It may not be used without prior written permission from Mesila's Jerusalem headquarters.

החוברת טעונה גניזה
Parts of this publication may require *genizah*.
Please do not discard.

Unit 1

Unit 2

Unit 3

Unit 4

Table of Contents

Introduction

Financial Stability and the Rest of Your Life

It's no secret that there are a lot of issues and challenges people are struggling with out there – many of which you are undoubtedly aware of.

All these diverse issues have to be dealt with. But there is one issue that may be at the root of all of them, or at least aggravating them: Financial stress. People are not managing to live with what they have, and the economic stress triggers all sorts of related problems.

When a family is already in the midst of a crisis, they can't deal with the root of the problem, because the symptoms are so urgent that they need to be dealt with on their own. But if you could turn the clock back and give people the tools to prevent them from getting into the financial stress to begin with, then you would avert not only the financial stress, but also all the other issues that go along with it.

The Mesila Course is what we call "preventative financial medicine." It is designed to give you the tools to manage your finances correctly from the onset and avoid financial pitfalls and missteps. "Next Steps," as the term implies, walks you out of the protected school/seminary environment and into the "real world." As you embark on this new stage, you want nothing more than to start off on the right foot. Mesila is here to provide you with the requisite knowledge, attitudes, and skills to lead a financially stable life in the years that lay ahead.

Financial literacy is taught in the general educational system around the world. However, the standard curriculum is often at odds – overtly or subtly – with the values that Torah promotes. In consideration of these unique sensitivities, Mesila has developed financial literacy curricula that presents the relevant material through the prism of Torah *hashkafah* and deals with the realities and challenges you are likely to face.

We hope this manual will infuse you with the confidence to do things right and trust you will find the content informative and enlightening.

Wishing you much hatzlacha!

Mesila Education Division

Units

Unit 1

Financial Stability and Attitudes Towards Money

What is Financial Stability?

Financial stability is the ability to handle your financial obligations in a way that contributes positively to other areas of your life. If you are financially stable, then you finances should enhance - not detract from - your health, your relationships, your quality of life, your peace of mind, and your ability to reach your life goals. This definition of financial stability views money as a tool, a means to a higher end, rather than as an end unto itself.

Financial stability is not a function of how much money you have. There are millionaires who suffer from terrible financial instability, because money is a source of tension and conflict in their lives, and there are low-income families who are models of financial stability, because they manage well with what they have and lead productive, happy lives, despite their meager means. Some of the main contributors to financial stability are the application of Torah values in dealing with money, correct financial attitudes, ability to prioritize, and the striving towards financial independence.

Goals

- To understand what financial stability is and why it's important
- To identify obstacles to financial stability
- To rank wants and needs in our lives
- To learn how to prioritize and make financially sound decisions
- To examine spending habits and grasp the concepts of opportunity cost and the time value of money
- To identify mistaken attitudes toward money and replace them with healthy attitudes.
- To recognize that Hashem gave us money to use charitably and with integrity
- To appreciate the value of achieving and maintaining financial independence
- To apply spending priorities and Torah attitudes into major spending decisions

STUDENT RESOURCE 1

MESILA'S GUIDELINES FOR FINANCIAL STABILITY

Charity & Financial Independence

1 Bailing people out of their financial predicaments almost guarantees that they will repeat their mistakes.

2 Although handouts, including government assistance, are necessary at times – to make sure that a person does not go hungry, for instance – it must be remembered that any time a person gets something for nothing it increases dependence and decreases motivation.

3 Accepting charity is a last resort and should be avoided if at all possible.

4 Taking charity is preferable to taking a loan without having a source from which to repay.

5 Financial independence is measured by degrees, and is not an all-or-nothing proposition. Every bit of improvement is significant.

Hishtadlus (Effort)

6 Success in any financial endeavor depends on *siyatta dishmaya*. But the fact that the outcome is in Hashem's hands does not absolve people of the obligation to invest the necessary effort into any enterprise they embark on.

7 From the time of Adam HaRishon, *parnassah* was meant to be difficult, and the fact that someone experiences difficulties does not mean he is doing anything wrong.

8 A person should always strive to improve his financial situation.

9 Every person has been endowed by Hashem with talents, skills or knowledge that can be used to generate income.

Risk

10 For every person, there is an appropriate level of financial risk, and it is important for every person to take certain risks.

11 There is no such thing as a no-risk venture.

Change

12 Lasting economic change happens naturally, from the ground up. It cannot be imposed on any person or community.

13 Sustainable long-term improvement in a person's financial situation is usually possible only if the person is actively involved in the change.

14 A person who does not want help cannot be helped. And no one can be forced to change his financial attitudes or habits.

15 As a means of achieving financial stability, increasing income is preferable to reducing expenditures, since reducing expenditures is liable to cause stress and friction in the home, and reductions are not always sustainable long-term.

16 Extreme financial measures do not last.

Counseling

17 A person should never be embarrassed to seek financial guidance.

18 When people are in the midst of difficult financial situations, they are often powerless to extricate themselves from their predicaments. A fresh pair of eyes is therefore immeasurably helpful.

Money & Possessions

19 Money is a means, not an end, and its importance must be kept in the correct proportion.

20 Money alone does not usually solve money problems.

21 There is no such thing as easy money.

22 No matter how high a standard of living a person maintains, there should always be things that he refuses himself and his children.

23 In any financial situation a person could possibly be in, there will be things that he will not be able to have.

Human Nature

24 People do not work with precise financial calculations; they work with estimates. And when estimating, the natural tendency is to err on the side that is more convenient.

25 Financial limitations create motivation. If a person feels limited to spending only what he has, he will be motivated to earn money so that he will have what to spend. But if a person gets used to borrowing money, his sense of financial limitation broadens to include all of the money he can potentially borrow, which decreases his motivation to earn money.

26 Financial structure creates freedom. In homes that run with a budget, money is generally less of an issue than in homes where spending limits are only loosely defined.

27 Expenses rise to meet income, because when funds are available, they find a destination. And when people's income rises, their needs rise, too – but their needs usually rise more than their income.

28 People prefer not to confront unpleasant realities.

29 The tendency is that people seek financial solutions outside of themselves, even though most viable solutions are found within their own resources.

Solutions to Financial Problems

30 Solutions to financial problems must be comprehensive, if they are to last. If even one contributing factor is not dealt with as part of the solution, the problem will likely fester and recur.

31 Flawed financial attitudes and habits are often a factor – and often the main factor – in financial difficulties, so the quest for comprehensive, lasting solutions must involve replacing these attitudes and habits with healthy ones.

32 Every person can be helped, and every financial situation can be improved, at least to some extent.

33 There are no instant or easy solutions to complex financial challenges.

34 Solutions are individual – what works for one person does not necessarily work for another.

Financial Management

35 It is incumbent upon every family to plan for their financial future and save up money to cover future needs.

36 Every drop adds up, and every little bit of money saved or earned is significant.

37 No person is perfect and no budget is perfect. Financial failure is a learning experience, not a reason to give up or abandon a budget.

38 No financial plan can be executed to perfection. But that is not a reason not to plan.

39 Financial management has to be based on the current situation as well as data from the past and future projections. But it cannot be based on nostalgia for the past or wishful thinking about the future.

40 Husband and wife have to work as a team in managing their finances and should not conceal financial information from one another.

41 Writing down budgetary data contributes to budgetary control and discipline and is a powerful financial management tool.

Children & Money

42 Children and teenagers need to have the security of knowing that their parents will provide all of their needs.

43 Children's needs are subjective, and depend very much on their environment.

44 Children do not need to know the details of what is happening with their parents' finances. The only time children should be made aware of what is happening with their parents' finances is when there is a change in the family's lifestyle that will affect them directly.

45 Money is a potent, intoxicating, and dangerous substance whose use by young children needs to be supervised and controlled.

46 The less involved parents are in their married children's finances, the better it is for everyone.

47 Supporting adult children is noble, but better than any money parents can give their adult children is the gift of financial independence.

MESILA'S GUIDELINES FOR FINANCIAL STABILITY

EXERCISE

INSTRUCTIONS: EACH OF THE FOLLOWING 20 SCENARIOS REFLECTS AN ATTITUDE THAT MIGHT LEAD TO FINANCIAL INSTABILITY. FOR EACH SCENARIO, CHOOSE ONE OF MESILA'S GUIDELINES FOR FINANCIAL STABILITY THAT YOU WOULD SUGGEST TO THE PERSON IN THE SCENARIO. NEXT TO EACH SCENARIO, WRITE THE NUMBER OF THE RELEVANT GUIDELINE.

1 | Mendy needs to make some cuts to his budget. He considers cutting out the coffee that he buys each morning, but then he thinks to himself, *Why should I bother? What difference is $2 a day going to make?* ?

2 | Ephraim is worried that his friend Aaron is falling further and further into debt because of financial mismanagement, and he suggests that Aaron apply to Mesila for help. When Aaron balks at the suggestion, Ephraim goes ahead and applies on his behalf. *Once the process has begun, Aaron will cooperate*, he thinks to himself. ?

3 | Esther sees an advertisement that says: "Work from home, two hours a day, earn up to $10,000 a month. No training or experience necessary. Just call 999-5555." ?

4 | Mr. Rosen works very hard as an accountant, putting in late hours and sweating over his clients' tax returns. "I must be doing something wrong," he says. "It shouldn't be this hard to earn a living." ?

5 | Elimelech and Rochel are a young couple whose generous parents have given them a credit card to use for all of their expenses, with no limitations and no questions asked. ?

6 | Yaakov's brother Refoel is a big spender who has amassed a large debt on his credit card. Yaakov decides to pay off Refoel's debt in order to give him a fresh start.

?

7 | Rivky is a secretary who is earning a bit more than minimum wage. She has been at the same position for almost ten years, and is satisfied with her job and her pay.

?

8 | Chaim is worried that his wife Dina will be upset if he tells her the details of their financial situation. He decides not to discuss it with her at all.

?

9 | "I don't understand why I run out of money every month," Simcha tells his Mesila counselor. "I'm earning $4,000, and spending $3,000, so why should I be having problems?"

?

10 | The Rosenberg family decides that in order to balance their budget, they will get rid of their cars and their cell phones and will not buy any new clothing for at least two years.

?

11 | Yossi opens a new business, without preparing a business plan, hiring a business consultant, or performing any market research. When his friend comments that he is being irresponsible, Yossi replies, "I have *bitachon* that Hashem will take care of the business for me."

?

12 | Avraham and Baila are an affluent couple who give their children whatever they ask for. "We can afford it, *baruch Hashem*," they say.

?

13 | Zev has been unemployed for a long time, and his savings have run out. He borrows money from a *gemach* to cover his living expenses, not knowing how he is going to pay it back. "It's better than accepting *tzedakah*," he says.

?

14 | "Just because everyone else in your class has that type of knapsack does not mean that you need it," Mrs. Gold tells her daughter. "I grew up without it, and you'll manage just fine without it, too."

?

15 | Yitzchak and Esty decide that it's silly to build a budget plan, because they have no way of knowing what their financial situation will be in the future. "A person never knows what will happen tomorrow," they say. "How do we know how much we'll be earning or spending in six months from now?"

?

16 | Berel tells his neighbor Avigdor that he managed to build a budget plan that solved all of his financial problems. "Can I have a copy of your plan?" Avigdor asks. "I'll follow it exactly."

?

17 | Bracha's boss gives her an unexpected raise. "Now we'll be able to trade in the car for a newer model," she tells her husband happily. "And we'll finally be able to finish the month."

?

18 | Yerachmiel was a successful businessman whose store was severely affected by the economic crisis, but he feels uncomfortable asking experienced businesspeople for advice.

?

19 | Mrs. Ehrlich is a widow with several young children who subsists off community support. "I would love to manage without *tzedakah*," she says, "but I know that's impossible. What point is there in trying to minimize the amount of *tzedakah* I take?"

?

20 | Shira just came back from seminary and has nothing to do. "Why should anyone want to give me a job?" she laments. "I have no skills and never did well in school."

?

STUDENT RESOURCE 2

MASLOW'S HIERARCHY OF NEEDS

(MODIFIED)

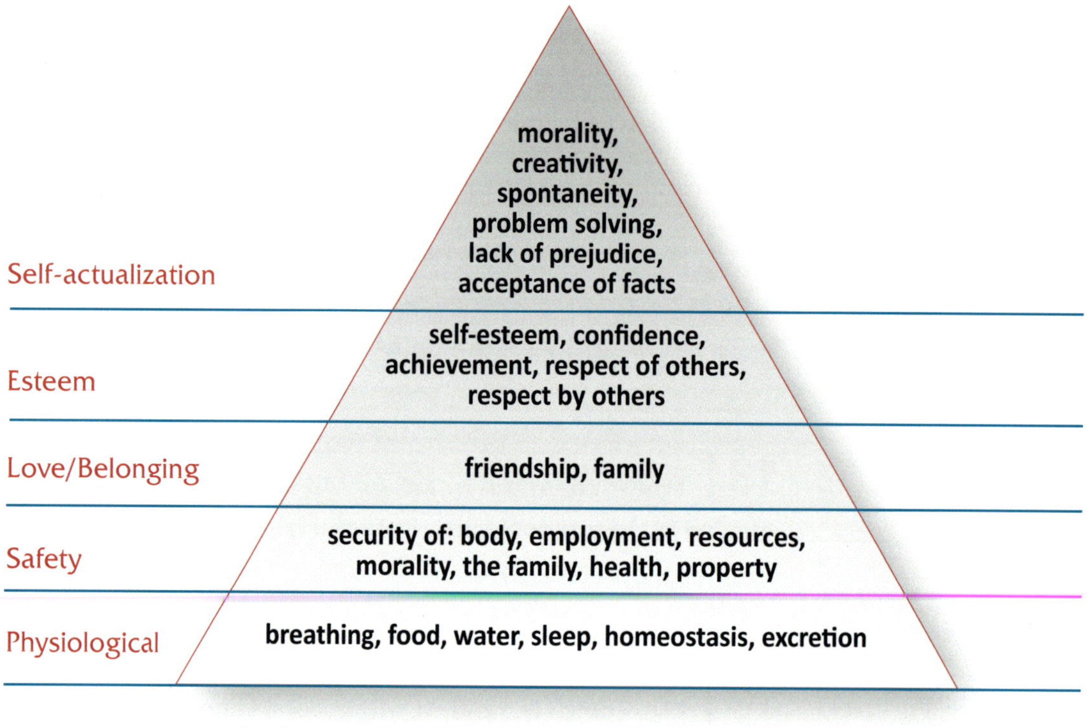

STUDENT RESOURCE 3

VALUES & VALUABLES

Every single hour of a woman's day is full of business decisions.
I remember when my children were small. And I had a million things to do. I did deals in my head – profits versus losses.
If they spill 6,000 Lego pieces all over the floor, but play quietly for a good hour, and it takes 10 minutes to sweep up the Lego, I've gained 50 minutes of free time....
Then there were the cumulative and non-cumulative cleaning calculations. For example, if you have an unusually busy schedule for the week, or life, what do you let go of and what not?
Cumulative chores are ones that build up. Like dishes, laundry, clutter. These will take the same amount of time if they are done immediately or left until later. Non-cumulative chores don't add up. A dirty floor takes the same amount of time to clean whether it's been dirty for three days or one.
Same sweeping motions, same time to cover floor space.
Life is a business.

From Mishpacha Magazine, Concentric Circles, by Esther Sender

Spending isn't only about money. Time and energy are other resources that we can spend - sometimes in place of money, sometimes in addition - and they also have value and need to be budgeted.

On the next page is a list of activities and pursuits that people in our communities typically devote time, energy, and money to.

Part 1:

Rank each of the following pursuits as Vital, Important, Not so important, or Not important at all.

Part 2:

Select your ten most important pursuits, and rank them in order of importance:

STUDENT RESOURCE 3

	Vital	Important	Not so important	Not important at all
Acquiring new skills				
Attending simchas				
Beauty treatments				
Car maintenance				
Charity				
Chessed & volunteering				
Cooking				
Correspondence (email, etc.)				
Davening				
Eating out				
Exercise				
Family outings				
Family time				
Gardening				
Gift-giving				
Going to *shiurim*				
Gourmet cooking/food decorating				
Grocery shopping				
Grooming				
Home redecorating				
Home maintenance				
Hosting guests				
Hosting parties (e.g., Sheva Berachos, parlor meetings)				
Landscaping				
Laundry				
Leisure & hobbies				
Music				
Nutrition				
Pet care				
Phone interaction with family & friends				
Photos				
Pleasure reading				
Recreational shopping				
Sleep				
Vacations & travel				
Wardrobe				
Weight loss				
Work responsibilities				
Other				
Other				

STUDENT RESOURCE 4

MONEY GAMES PEOPLE PLAY

Negative Games: Illusion or Reality?

A. CHARADES

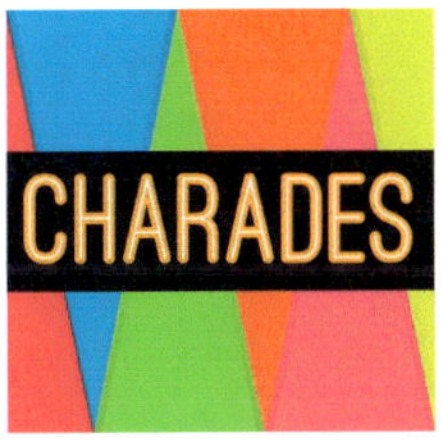

Charades is basically putting on an act to make people think that you are something that you're not. When people spend money to create an illusory image to impress other people, rather than spending it on things they need and want - they are actually playing a game of Charades.

שפת תמים להחפץ חיים פרק ה'

"**שבתחלה** כשהקב"ה מזמין לאדם מעות בחסדו, כדי שיוכל להחיות את נפשו בזה, וגם לפרוע מזה חובות הבורא כצדקה וגמ"ח והחזקת התורה, וכדומה לזה. היצה"ר מסיתו, שעתה נאות לו להתנהג בעניני הוצאות הבית והמלבושים במעלה הגבוה מערכו והפחות כהמכובד, והמכובד כאחד מעשירי העם. כדי שיתראה לחשוב ומכובד לעיני חביריו. והאדם הולך אחר עצתו, מרגיל את עצמו בזה, עד שבהמשך הזמן הוא נעשה מוכרח לזה להתנהג כדרך הגבוהים."

At first Hashem, in his kindness, gives a person money, so that he can use it to support himself, as well as to carry out his spiritual obligations, such as by giving *tzedakah*, lending money, and supporting Torah. But the Yetzer Hara persuades him that it would now be appropriate to raise his standards of spending on his home and wardrobe to match his new station - the lowly person [tries to be] like the more dignified one, and the dignified one, like the rich - in order to appear more important and respectable in the view of his friends. The person follows the Yetzer Hara's advice and accustoms himself to this new standard, until he feels compelled to act as though he is wealthy.

B. UNO

In this game, whoever is left with the fewest cards at the end wins.

This game is played by the opposite personality of the one who plays CHARADES. Here we are speaking of a person who takes pride in how little she has and what she manages without. (But sometimes, the same person will play both games at different times.)

Simplicity is definitely a virtue. But at the same time, ignoring Hashem's gifts to us and presenting ourselves as a "*nebach*" shows a lack of *hakaras hatov* and is not a Torah value.

דברים ב, ז

"כי ה' אלקיך ברכך" - לפיכך לא תכפו (ס"א תכפרו) את טובתו להראות כאילו אתם עניים אלא הראו עצמכם עשירים (רש"י).

"Because Hashem your G-d has blessed you" Devarim 2:7

Rashi - Therefore do not be ungrateful (to Hashem) by presenting yourself as poor but rather present yourself as wealthy.

C. CANDYLAND

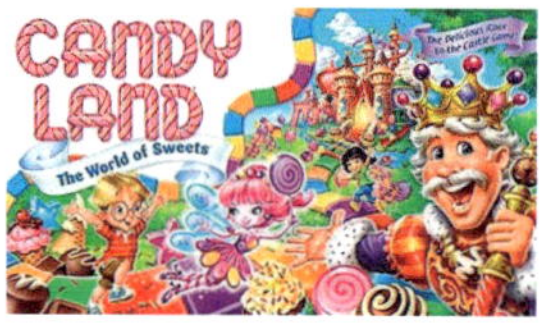

Remember when you were a kid and played Candyland? You entered this magical world, with princesses and lots of candy and bright colors. Now think: Isn't that the feeling you have when you've had a bad day and then you step into a mall? It's a great escape into Fantasy Land - Everyone is smiling, everything's pretty and colorful and attractively arranged, with dazzling displays, tantalizing smells, pleasant background music, salespeople fawning over you...

But is it real? As you empty your wallet and swipe your credit card, are you living life, or are you "playing Candyland," trying to buy an illusory experience?

D. TABOO

You get a card with a word that needs to be explained, as well as a list of other words that you may not use in your explanation. You end up talking around those words in order to make yourself understood.

People don't speak openly to themselves. They can't face what is really going on. It's fine to refrain from talking about your private money matters to others, as long as you, personally, can face the issues head on. But when someone goes to great lengths to whitewash money issues even in his own mind, he is avoiding facing the music on all levels.

E. BELTS

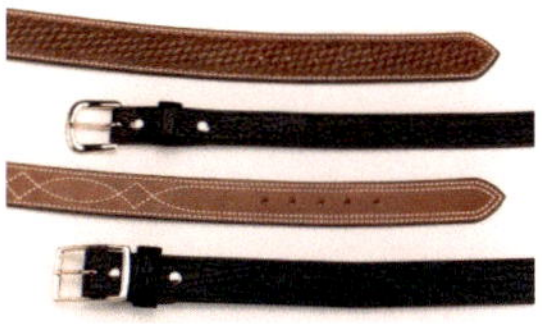

Two belts are put at a distance from each other, and each player jumps over them with a predetermined number of leaps. The last jump determines where the second belt will be moved to, setting the outer limit for the next round.

Here's a more grown-up version of belts. Everyone comes to a Shabbaton thinking she looks nice. Then someone walks in with her new designer shoes and "moves the belt." Suddenly, everyone else feels that she has to upgrade her wardrobe a notch in order to keep up. Otherwise, "I lost."

The same is true later in life, with cars and weddings and kitchens; there's always someone who's going to take a longer leap than you and raise the bar beyond your reach. Are you going to play the game and make a superhuman effort to keep up?

What do all these games - Charades, Uno, Candyland, and Belts - have in common?

These games are all "virtual living." Does your life reflect who you really are and what you really have? Or are you living a "make-believe life" - pretending to others, and even to yourself?

The Real Thing: Positive Games That People Play

A. SOLITAIRE

Solitaire is a game that you play by yourself. You win, or you lose - but only because of what you choose to do; you are the only player.

Similarly, finances should be an independent, personal process for each person. Different people have differing needs and wants. A person has to establish his own needs and priorities, independent of those of the people around him.

This is the idea of די מחסורו - providing a person with what he lacks, though for someone else it may be a luxury. Needs and wants are intricately connected to a person's upbringing, personality, and the society he lives in, and "rich" and "poor" are relative, not absolute, terms.

STUDENT
RESOURCE
4

דברים טו, ח

"כִּי פָתֹחַ תִּפְתַּח אֶת יָדְךָ לוֹ וְהַעֲבֵט תַּעֲבִיטֶנּוּ דֵּי מַחְסֹרוֹ אֲשֶׁר יֶחְסַר לוֹ".

Rather you shall open your hand to him and you shall lend him sufficiently for his needs which he is lacking.

רמב"ם הלכות מתנות עניים ז:ג

"לפי מה שחסר העני אתה מצווה ליתן לו אם אין לו כסות מכסים אותו אם אין לו כלי בית קונין לו אם אין לו אשה משיאין אותו ואם היתה אשה משיאין אותה לאיש אפילו היה דרכו של זה העני לרכוב על הסוס ועבד רץ לפניו והעני וירד מנכסיו קונין לו סוס לרכוב עליו ועבד לרוץ לפניו שנאמר די מחסורו אשר יחסר לו.

We are commanded to give a poor person according to what he lacks. If he lacks clothes, we should clothe him. If he lacks household utensils, we should purchase them for him. If he is unmarried, we should help him marry. And for an unmarried woman, we should find a husband for her.

Even if the personal habit of this poor person was to ride on a horse and to have a servant run before him and then he became impoverished and lost his wealth, we should buy a horse for him to ride and a servant to run before him. [This is implied by *Devarim* 15:8 which] speaks [of providing him with] "enough to [fill the] lack that he feels." You are commanded to fill his lack, but you are not obligated to enrich him.

B. PAPER BAG DRAMATICS

In this game, each player gets a paper bag with a random assortment of 10 items and has to put on a skit using all the items in the bag.

Every Rosh Hashanah, Hashem gives you your "bag of objects" - your resources for the upcoming year.

Make sure that you use whatever is in your bag wisely; it cannot be refilled or exchanged!

ביצה טז.

"כל מזונותיו של אדם קצובים לו מראש השנה ועד יום הכפורים.

From Rosh Hashanah to Yom Kippur, a person's entire livelihood is allotted to him.

רש"י

כל מזונותיו של אדם - כל מה שעתיד להשתכר בשנה, שיהא נזון משם קצוב לו, כך וכך ישתכר בשנה זו, ויש לו ליזהר מלעשות יציאה מרובה שלא יוסיפו לו שכר למזונות אלא מה שפסקו לו:

A person's entire livelihood - all that he will earn in the coming year to support himself is set aside for him, such is the amount he will earn this year. He must take care not to spend too much as no more support will be added other than that was already decided for him.

There are many different levels of finances - many types of "paper bags." But most people can manage with what they get, be it more or less. We're not talking now about people who are truly poor or are in unusual medical or other circumstances; we're talking about regular people. Even those who struggle financially can use what they have to cover their needs. It's all a question of budgeting.

Hashem gives everyone what he needs to accomplish his life's mission. Our job is to use what we are given in the best possible way.

C. DOMINOES

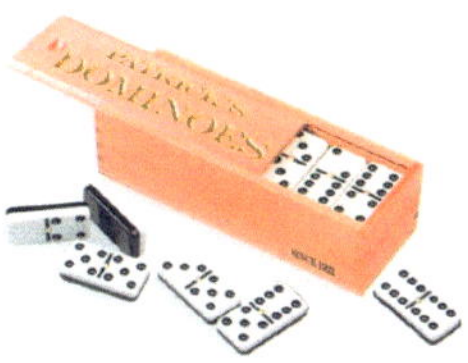

This game is the opposite of Candyland, in which you disconnect from the real world and temporarily enter a fantasy world. In dominoes, we see our finances as a lineup of standing dominoes. If we knock one over by making a financial misstep, it has the domino effect of knocking all the rest out of place.

Every dollar in your pocket is connected to the one before it and the one after it, like dominoes. No spending decision occurs in a vacuum. If I buy this, I won't be able to buy that. If I don't buy this, I'll have money left for something else.

STUDENT RESOURCE 5

CHARITY & PHILANTHROPY: AN ETHICAL IMPERATIVE

1. Charity is a Torah commandment emphasized repeatedly in Tanach.

כִּי יִהְיֶה בְךָ אֶבְיוֹן מֵאַחַד אַחֶיךָ בְּאַחַד שְׁעָרֶיךָ בְּאַרְצְךָ אֲשֶׁר ה' אֱלֹקֶיךָ נֹתֵן לָךְ לֹא תְאַמֵּץ אֶת לְבָבְךָ וְלֹא תִקְפֹּץ אֶת יָדְךָ מֵאָחִיךָ הָאֶבְיוֹן. כִּי פָתֹחַ תִּפְתַּח אֶת יָדְךָ לוֹ וְהַעֲבֵט תַּעֲבִיטֶנּוּ דֵּי מַחְסֹרוֹ אֲשֶׁר יֶחְסַר לוֹ... כִּי לֹא יֶחְדַּל אֶבְיוֹן מִקֶּרֶב הָאָרֶץ עַל כֵּן אָנֹכִי מְצַוְּךָ לֵאמֹר פָּתֹחַ תִּפְתַּח אֶת יָדְךָ לְאָחִיךָ לַעֲנִיֶּךָ וּלְאֶבְיֹנְךָ בְּאַרְצֶךָ:

If there will be among you a pauper from one of your brothers in one of your gates in your land that Hashem your God is giving you, you shall not harden your hard and you shall not close your hand from your impoverished brother. Rather, you shall surely open your hand to him and you shall lend him what he requires, whatever is lacking to him...For there will not cease to be a pauper in the midst of the land. Therefore I am commanding you saying, You shall surely open your hand to your brother to your poor and to your impoverished in your land.

(Devarim 15)

2. Hashem provides for everyone, but the distribution is unequal - some people have more than they need while some have less. Why? Because He wants to give His people the merit of giving to others (*Sefer HaChinuch* 66).

שרצה הקֵל להיות ברואיו מלומדים ומורגלים במדת החסד והרחמים, כי היא מדה משובחת... ואם לאו מצד שורש זה הלא הוא ברוך הוא יספיק לעני די מחסורו זולתנו, אלא שהיה מחסדו ברוך הוא שנעשינו שלוחים לו לזכותנו.

Hashem wished to accustom humanity in the qualities of kindness and compassion, for those are exemplary qualities...If not for this underlying consideration, Hashem would provide for the pauper without us. But in His kindness, He made us His emissaries, in order for us to accrue merit.

3. Sharing one's resources with others is not merely meritorious - it is an absolute obligation. In fact, the reason that some people have more and some people have less is because Hashem expects people to take responsibility for the poor and indigent and ensure that their needs are met as well.

Ohr Hachaim on the verse אִם כֶּסֶף תַּלְוֶה אֶת עַמִּי - *When you will lend money to my people* (*Shemos* 22:24):

אם כסף תלוה את עמי פירוש אם ראית שהיה לך כסף יותר על מה שאתה צריך לעצמך, שאתה מלוה לעמי, תדע לך שאין זה חלק המגיעך, אלא חלק אחרים שהוא העני עמך, ובזה רמז כי צריך לפתוח לו משלו ואולי כי רמז לו גם כן שלא יתנשא ויתגדל על העני, בראותו כי הוא הנותן לו, והוא אומרו לא תהיה לו כנושה, לשון נשיאות ומעלה, כי משלו הוא נותן לו.

The verse "When you will lend money to my people" means: If you see that you have more money than you require for yourself, and that you are able to lend to others, you should know that this is not your portion to which you are entitled, but rather the portion of others - namely, the pauper among you. With this, the Torah insinuates that a person must open to the pauper of his [the pauper's] own resources, and perhaps it is also intimating that he should not act condescendingly or arrogantly toward the pauper when he sees that he is the one giving to the pauper. That is the meaning of the verse, You shall not be as a creditor (nosheh) to him, nosheh being related to the word for haughtiness (nesius), for he is giving the pauper what rightfully belongs to him (the pauper).

---

4. When carrying out your responsibility to provide for others in need, realize that they are doing you a bigger favor than you are doing for them. For you are providing them with mere money or material assistance, while they are providing you with eternal merit. (*Vayikra Raba* 34:8)

יותר ממה שבעל הבית עושה עם העני, העני עושה עם בעל הבית שכן רות אומרת לנעמי (רות ב) שם האיש אשר עשיתי עמו היום בועז אשר עשה עמי אין כתיב כאן אלא אשר עשיתי עמו.

More than the householder does for the pauper, the pauper does for the householder, as Rus said to Naomi, "The name of the man for whom I did today is Boaz." The verse does not say "who did for me" but rather "for whom I did."

[In other words, Rus was implying that she did something for Boaz, though it would seem that he had given to her.]

STUDENT RESOURCE 6

MAASER AND CHOMESH: A TENTH AND A FIFTH

***Maaser*: A tenth**

1. From the time of Avraham, Yitzchak, and Yaakov, Jews have traditionally tithed their produce and income.
2. The minimum tithe is 1/10; the maximum is 1/5.
3. *Maseches Kesuvos* 50:

המבזבז אל יבזבז יותר מחומש שמא יצטרך לבריות.

One who dispenses [charity] should not dispense more than a fifth [of his money], lest he become dependent on others.

---

4. Exceptions to this 1/5 limitation (Source - *Ahavas Chessed* 20):
   - (a) A person on his deathbed (there's no danger that he'll become dependent on society)
   - (b) A very wealthy person
   - (c) When hungry and indigent people approach the donor for help he has to feed and clothe them
   - (d) When the recipient's life is in danger
   - (e) For the support of Torah study
5. Possible uses for maaser money
   - (1) Some say it must be used for charity
   - (2) Others say it may be used for other mitzvos as well; ask a rabbi

STUDENT RESOURCE 7

PRIORITIES IN CHARITY

1. **Yourself**
   a. חייך קודמים - Your life comes first (*Bava Metzia* 62a)
   b. פרנסת עצמו קודמת לכל אדם - Providing for oneself takes precedence over anyone else (*Rema, Yoreh Deah* 251:3)
   c. “Put on your own oxygen mask before assisting other passengers”
   d. Clearly, this applies to one’s basic needs, not to extravagances.

2. **Your family: Charity begins at home**
   a. וּמִבְּשָׂרְךָ לֹא תִתְעַלָּם - And to your own flesh, you shall not be oblivious (*Yeshayah* 58:7)
   b. עניי ביתו קודמין לעניי עירו - The poor of one’s household [i.e., one’s family] take precedence over the poor of one’s city (*Shulchan Aruch Yoreh Deah* 251:3)

3. **Torah scholars** (enabling their Torah study).

מהנכון שיהדר לכתחילה לחלקם לעמלי תורה למען יחזקו בעבודת ה' כי משמע במדרש דעיקר המעשר נתקן בשביל להחזיק לעמלי תורה.

It is proper, most ideally, to distribute charity to those who study Torah, in order that they be strengthened in their Divine service, for it is understood from the Midrash that the requirement of maaser was instituted primarily in order to support those who study Torah.

---

4. **Other paupers**
   Examples of other categories of precedence in giving charity:
   a. The needy of one’s city and the needy of the Land of Israel come before other needy individuals
   b. A Kohen or Levi comes before a Yisrael
   c. Parents come before other relatives (including adult children)
   d. Food over clothing
   e. Needy woman over needy man

STUDENT RESOURCE 8

THE MITZVAH OF LENDING

מצות עשה מן התורה להלוות לעניי אחינו, שנאמר (שמות כב, כד) אם כסף תלוה את עמי את העני עמך גו'. ואיתא במכילתא דכל "אם" שבתורה רשות, ושלושה מהן חובה, וזה אחד מהן. וראיה ממה שאמר הכתוב "והעבט תעביטנו" דרך ציווי. ומצוה זו גדולה יותר ממצות הצדקה, שאין העני בוש בדבר כל כך. גם שבזה תומך ידו ומחזיק אותו שלא יתמוטט לגמרי, ומקיים בזה מה שאמר הכתוב (ויקרא כה, לה) וכי ימוך אחיך ומטה ידו עמך, והחזקת בו וגו' דהיינו שיחזיק בו עד שלא יפול ויצטרך לבריות. ומצוה גם כן להלוות לעשיר לפי שעה [היינו לזמן מועט] בשעה שאין המעות מצוי לו, דגמילות חסד נוהג בין לעניים בין לעשירים. אלא דהעני קודם לו בזה, ולכך פירט הכתוב לעני במצוה זו. ואי לא דהודיענו הכתוב, היה רצונו של אדם יותר להלוות לעשיר, מפני שגם הוא ישיג פעמים רבות טובות ממנו, ועוד שהעשיר בטוח אצלו יותר. ודע עוד, דלאו דווקא הלוואת מעות, דהוא הדין דמצוה להשאיל לו כליו ושאר חפציו כיוצא בזה.

It is a positive commandment from the Torah to lend to our impoverished brethren, as the verse states (Shemos 22:24), "When (im) you will lend money to my nation, to the pauper among you...." It is brought in the Mechilta that all instances of the word "im" in the Torah relate to optional actions, but three are obligations, and this is one of them. The proof to this is the Torah's statement "You shall surely lend to him," which is a direct commandment. This mitzvah is even greater than the mitzvah of charity, for the pauper is not as ashamed [when receiving a loan, as opposed to charity]. In lending a pauper money, one also supports his hand and strengthens him so that he should not collapse entirely, in fulfillment of the verse (Vayikra 25:35), "If your brother becomes impoverished and his hand falters near you, you shall strengthen him..." meaning that he should strengthen him to the point that he will not collapse and become dependent on others. It is also a mitzvah to lend to a wealthy person temporarily, at a time when he does not have money available, for the mitzvah of chessed applies to poor and rich alike, except that the pauper takes precedence over the wealthy person; that is why the verse specified the pauper in this commandment. Had the Torah not told us this, a person would have preferred to lend to the wealthy person, because he himself can often receive benefit from him, and also because he is more confident in the wealthy person. Furthermore, the mitzvah is not limited to lending money, for the halachah is that it is a mitzvah to lend a person his utensils and other objects and the like.

STUDENT RESOURCE 9

INTEGRITY

1. Chazal tell us that the majority of people are tainted by theft (Bava Basra 165:a):

אמר רב יהודה אמר רב, רוב בגזל

Rav Yehudah said in the name of Rav: Most [people are guilty] of theft.

2. A person never profits from lack of integrity (*sefer Chassidim*, 1075-1076).

המלוה בריבית, ממונו יכלה, או הגוזז מעות וכן העושה עולה במשקל במדה ובמשורה ובסחורות ובכל מיני עולה, לבסוף ירדו מנכסיהם, ובניהם יתפרדו זה מזה בארץ נכריה, ונצרכים לבריות. וגם כל שיהיו חביריהם וכל הנלוה אליהם יכלה ממונם, וכל שיהיה מסייע להם.

One who lends with interest, his money will be wiped out; as well as one who embezzles money, or cheats in weights, measures, merchandise or any other fraud. Eventually, they will lose their money, and their children will be estranged from one another in a foreign land and be dependent on others. In addition, all those who befriend these [unscrupulous] people and all those who are attached to them, their money will be wiped out. The same will happen to alll those who facilitate them.

STUDENT RESOURCE 10

THE TORAH VIEW OF FINANCIAL DEPENDENCE

1. *Birkas Hamazon*:

ונא אל תצריכנו ה' אלקינו לא לידי מתנת בשר ודם ולא לידי הלוואתם.

Please do not make us needy of the gifts of human hands nor of their loans.

2. *Maseches Beitza* 32:

כל המצפה על שלחן אחרים עולם חשך בעדו... רב חסדא אמר אף חייו אינן חיים.

One who depends on others for sustenance, the world is dark for him...Rav Chisda says: In addition, his life is not a life.

a. *Chasam Sofer*:

והוסיף רב חסדא גם חייו בעה"ב אינם חיים כי כיון שלא זכה ליהנות מיגיע כפו דכתיב גביה אשריך בעה"ז וטוב לך לעה"ב וזה הוא ההיפך משניהם. אבל ת"ח איננו בגדר מצפה על שולחן אחרים, אלא בגדר ועמדו אחרים ורעו צאנכם, וק"ל:

b. Explanation of Chasam Sofer: What Rav Chisda is adding with his statement that "His life is not a life" is that his life *in the next world* is not a life, because he did not benefit from his own efforts, as the Talmud teaches that one who benefits from his own efforts is fortunate in both this world and the next world. However, a *talmid chacham* is not considered one who depends on others for sustenance; rather, because he is engaged in Torah study, he deserves to be freed from mundane matters (see *Berachos* 35b).

3. Jewish law mandates that a person go to great lengths to avoid being financially dependent (*Tur Yoreh Deah* 255:1-2).

לעולם ירחיק אדם עצמו מהצדקה ויגלגל עצמו בצער שלא יצטרך לבריות וכן צוו חכמים עשה שבתך חול ואל תצטרך לבריות.

A person should always distance himself from charity and subject himself to affliction rather than being dependent on others, as the Sages instructed, "Make your Shabbos a weekday rather than be dependent on others."

STUDENT RESOURCE 11

TAKING CHARITY ON A ONE-TIME BASIS

Question: *I work as a sofer, and I earn a modest income that is usually enough to cover my family's needs on a month-by-month basis. I have never earned much money, but I also never thought of myself as "poor." Several months ago, I injured my wrist, and I was sidelined from work for about a month. During that period, I had no choice but to borrow money from a gemach and from a couple of friends in order to live. Now, I am baruch Hashem able to work again, but I am left with a considerable amount of debt that I do not see how I can repay. A local tzedakah organization is aware of my financial plight, and they offered me a one-time grant to pay off my debts and put me back onto my feet.*

To me, taking tzedakah is anathema, and I would like to avoid it at all costs. But I honestly don't really see any option at this point. I am considering applying for Mesila's services, but because you do not give people tzedakah, I am not sure that you can help me. Is there anything Mesila can do for me?

A: You are to be commended for your reluctance to take tzedakah money. Jews have always gone to great lengths to avoid taking alms, and for good reason. The Gemara (*Beitzah* 32b) says about a person who depends on others for sustenance that the world is dark for him, and that his life is not life. Obviously, taking tzedakah money is something that the Torah views as a last resort, and something that should be avoided if at all possible.

Lehavdil, in the world of economics, evidence abounds that welfare programs actually increase dependency and perpetuate poverty. When people get money for doing nothing, they invariably lose some of their motivation to work for money. This is a psychological reality that is difficult to overcome.

If you were to accept tzedakah, even if only on a one-time basis, you will have crossed the line from financial independence to dependency. And once you cross that line, it will become far more difficult for you to refrain from accepting tzedakah again.

You write that Mesila does not give people tzedakah. It is true that in most cases we do not give out tzedakah *money*, but we actually do give people tzedakah. The highest form of tzedakah, according to the Rambam and the *Shulchan Aruch*, is helping a person become self-sufficient and not need to take money from others. The counseling services we provide put people on their feet while preserving their dignity and financial independence.

In Mesila's ten years of working with families experiencing financial difficulties – and these, by the way, are not limited to "poor" families – we have found that money is not necessarily the solution to financial problems. Financial problems are usually the result of lack of knowledge and poor financial management skills. By helping people to acquire the necessary knowledge and financial management skills, Mesila has helped hundreds of families and businesses to solve their financial problems.

The fact that some tzedakah organizations today are beginning to offer Mesila-style counseling services is an indication that more and more people are realizing that very often, money alone will not solve financial problems. In your case specifically, taking tzedakah on a one-time basis might cover your shortfall for the time being, but it will not prevent a similar crisis from recurring in the future. It also establishes a dangerous precedent.

Let's face it: living from month to month leaves you little financial breathing room, and you could easily land up in debt again in the future. This is not a pessimistic view of your situation; it is a realistic assessment.

If there is a Mesila branch in your community, we encourage you to apply for our counseling services. Mesila can help you develop a budget that will allow you to cover your living expenses, pay off your debts (slowly, if necessary), and save up money for unforeseen expenses or "rainy day" situations such as an injured wrist. (Mesila includes unforeseen expenses in the category of foreseeable expenses. Smart budgeting always takes rainy days into account.)

A Mesila counselor can also help you find ways to increase your income and decrease your expenditures. This will give you the financial breathing room that will allow you to ride out minor financial crises that may arise in the future.

The Gemara (*Berachos* 5b) observes that "*Ein chavush matir atzmo mibeis ha'asurim*" – a prisoner cannot release himself from prison. When people are in the midst of difficult situations, they often are powerless to extricate themselves from their predicaments. This principle is extremely applicable to people going through financial difficulties. Even if you are a financially responsible person, you might find it extremely beneficial to have a resourceful, experienced, and objective Mesila counselor tackling your financial issues together with you.

Before applying to Mesila, however, be aware that our counseling services are far-reaching and very thorough. Helping a family achieve financial stability is not something that can be accomplished overnight, and it takes months, and sometimes years, of counseling before the family becomes fully self-sufficient.

If there is no Mesila branch in your area, then we would recommend that you take the tzedakah offered to you, but that you try to view it as a loan, not as a handout. You can then slowly save up money to repay the "loan." When you save up enough money, you can make a donation to the organization that gave you the money. In this way, you can avoid the stigma of taking tzedakah.

If your local tzedakah organization offers any type of counseling, we strongly encourage you to accept it. These counseling services may not be as comprehensive or as structured as Mesila's, but they are certainly helpful nonetheless.

The Mishnah (*Pe'ah* 8:9) says that if a person needs tzedakah but refrains from taking it, he will eventually be able to support others with his own money. Although this mishnah does not apply to someone who is unable to survive without taking tzedakah, we believe that in your case it probably does apply. If you can find a way out to avoid taking tzedakah, you will reap the benefits of remaining financially independent in both this world and the next.

STUDENT RESOURCE 12

LET'S PLAN A WEDDING!

Maximum limit: 1000 points

Note: You must choose at least 300 points worth of items on right column.

ITEM	FIRST CHOICE	SECOND CHOICE	THIRD CHOICE
Shabbos Shaitel	72 points pre-cut out of the box	98 points medium custom	125 points top custom
Every-day shaitel	69 points pre-cut out of the box	86 points medium custom	120 points top custom
Wedding dress	25 points borrow or gemach	77 points rental	140 points new, made for you
Flowers	45 points Gemach centerpieces and fresh arrangement for Kallah	76 points Fresh flowers for center pieces and arrangement for Kallah	122 points Top of the line stunning arrangements with all the extras
Makeup and hair specialist	25 points I'll pass - I have a friend who's good	42 points Yes - for the Kallah	90 points Yes - for the whole wedding party
Caterer	115 points Simple	170 points Better than average	250 points All the trimmings
Music	60 points One man band including vocals	84 points Three piece band including vocals	120 points 5 top musicians
Photographer	60 points 1 Photographer, 1 videographer	86 points 1 photographer for men, plus one for women, 1 videographer for men plus one for women - but low end cost	112 points High end team for men and women - nothing gets missed!

Pre-Chuppa	58 points light buffet with 2 hot dishes for women, kabbalas panim for men	82 points 4 hot dishes plus buffet - for women and men	117 points deluxe blow-out shmorg
Dessert	50 points each person received a basic dessert	66 points extra nice dessert and cake and coffee in addition	105 points Viennese table
Sheva Brachos outfits	50 points 2 should do it - I have from dating	88 points four - I'll double if I need to	130 points somethng for every night plus three for Shabbos
Gifts for the chassan over engagemnt period	62 points standard chassan Shas and decent watch	78 points deluxe Shas (the kind thats too big to be used) and really nice watch	105 points deluxe Shas with gold inlay, designer watch, plus silver esrog box or megilla and expensive cuff links...

Unit 2

Budgeting and Money Management

Introduction

Budgeting means managing any type of limited resource - in this case, money. We all have limited money at our disposal; the challenge is to use our money in a way that will bring us maximum benefit and cause us minimal financial stress.

The idea of budgeting makes many people tense, because they automatically associate "budgeting" with "I can't afford what I want." But budgeting is not about restrictions, it's about the control that comes with awareness. Budgeting gives you control over your finances, freeing you to use your money as you see fit. Your budget doesn't tell you how to spend your money - *You tell your budget how you want to spend your money!*

Some people misunderstand the concept of *bitachon* and mistakenly regard budgeting as being counter to trust in Hashem, but our sources assert otherwise. Maintaining orderly finances is a Torah imperative.

Goals

- To understand what a budget is and why it's necessary to have one
- To examine the Torah sources regarding the value of budgeting
- To appreciate the role budgeting plays in enabling us to frame our goals
- To learn how to deal with budgeting and meeting children's needs and wants
- To appreciate importance of enhancing income, alongside streamlining expenses

At the end of the Student Book, we have provided the full handbook, "Mesila's Student Guide to Budgeting. The goals of this self-contained section are as follows:

- To learn how to keep finances orderly by distinguishing between the various aspects of one's finances
- To learn how to track income and expenses, large and small
- To take into consideration annual and unanticipated expenses, in addition to monthly outlays
- To explain the concept of cash flow and learn how to build a cash flow plan
- To practice building a real budget
- To appreciate the value of downsizing

STUDENT RESOURCE 13

TORAH VIEW ON BUDGETING

1 | ביצה טז.

כל מזונותיו של אדם קצובים לו מראש השנה ועד יום הכיפורים חוץ מהוצאת שבתות והוצאת יום טוב והוצאת בניו לתלמוד תורה שאם פחת פוחתין לו ואם הוסיף מוסיפין לו.

All of a person's [annual] mezonos is decreed upon him between Rosh Hashanah and Yom Kippur, with the exception of Shabbos expenses, Yom Tov expenses, and expenses for chinuch of his children. For those items, if he skimps, his income is reduced, and if he adds, his income is increased.

רש"י שם

כל מזונותיו של אדם - כל מה שעתיד להשתכר בשנה, שיהא נזון משם קצוב לו, כך וכך ישתכר בשנה זו, ויש לו ליזהר מלעשות יציאה מרובה שלא יוסיפו לו שכר למזונות אלא מה שפסקו לו:

All of a person's mezonos - this refers to what he is destined to earn that year, from which he shall be sustained. That amount is decreed for him - x is what he will earn this year. Therefore, he should be careful not to overspend, since no income will be added to his mezonos beyond what was ruled for him.

2 | ספר החינוך פרשת ויקרא מצוה קכ"ג מצוות קרבן עולה ויורד

בקטע המתחיל מדיני המצוה כתוב בזה הלשון:

שכל אחד מארבע חטאים אלה מחייב עושהו להביא כשבה או שעירה כדין חטאת קבועה הידוע, ואינו נפטר בעוף או בקמח אלא אם כן הוא עני.

ואם הוא עני והביא כשבה או שעירה לא יצא ידי חובתו.

והטעם לפי שאחר שהקל ברוך הוא ריחם עליו ופטרו בכך אינו בדין שידחק עצמו להביא יותר ממה שתשיג ידו.

ובזה יקנה כל מבין עצה לבלתי עשות הוצאות ביותר מן הראוי לו לפי ממונו, יען כי בו סיבה לגזול את הבריות כשמבקש לימודו ואינו מוצא.

In the section explaining the laws of the mitzvah, it says as follows:
Each one of these four sins requires the one who committed it to bring a sheep or goat, like the law of a regular chatas offering. A person cannot absolve himself of this obligation with a bird or flour unless he is poor.
If he is poor, and [rather than bring a simple offering that he can afford] he brings [the more costly] sheep or goat, he has not met his requirement.
The reason is that since Hashem has absolved him [from the more costly offering] it is inappropriate that he pressure himself to bring more than he can afford.
From this, the insightful person should learn not to incur greater expenses than are appropriate for him, based on the money that he has, as this may cause him to steal from others, when he cannot otherwise keep up to the standard to which he has become accustomed.

3 | הגריעב"ץ - הנהגת משא ומתן

עיין בהוצאה לעומת הכנסה... וסדר הוצאה הוא חצי פרנסה.

Examine your spending and how it corresponds to your income...You will find that organizing expenses is [equal to] half a salary.

4 | השל"ה הקדוש

מכל מקום יש ללמוד ממנו שיעיין האדם בכל אשר לו, ואם אינו בכל יום, מכל מקום יקבע בכל חדש יום אחד, וגם יתבונן במשא ומתן שלו, ואם רואה שההוצאה שלו היא יותר מהריוח שמרויח, יתבונן לצמצם כדי שלא יתמוטט.

In any case, one should learn from this that a person should review everything he owns, if not every day, then at least one day each month. He should review his business dealings, and if he sees that his expenses exceed his income, he should reduce his expenses to avoid collapse.

STUDENT RESOURCE 14

MONEY, HAPPINESS AND BUNNY RABBITS

Q: *For many years, my husband earned a six-figure salary working for a prestigious financial institution. His company was hit hard by the crisis, and had to downsize drastically. My husband, who is a senior employee, was offered the choice of being laid off and receiving a mediocre severance package, or continuing to work for the company at a greatly reduced salary. The prospect of unemployment was not one that we were prepared to face, so we chose the latter option.*

My husband's salary is still sufficient to live on, but it is not nearly enough to support the type of lifestyle our family is accustomed to. It looks as though we will have to sell our second car, cancel our planned family vacation to Switzerland, and eliminate the children's art and music lessons. I have also become much more careful about spending. I never used to look at prices when I went shopping – I just bought whatever I needed. Now, shopping is torture for me, because I always have to think twice before I buy anything.

Cutting down our expenses has been a bitter pill to swallow. I suppose I should be grateful that we can still pay our bills, but I find myself focusing much more on the things that are now lacking in my life. How can I cope with this situation – and help my children cope – without feeling deprived and bitter?

A: *Kol hakavod* to you and your husband for acknowledging your financial reality and for your readiness to make the necessary modifications to your lifestyle. Many formerly prosperous individuals are too accustomed to their former way of life, or too afraid of what other people will think, to adjust their lifestyle to their means. Instead, they are attempting to maintain their previous standard of living, with disastrous results.

It is never easy for a family to lower its standard of living, and that is why Mesila tries to avoid telling families to reduce their spending. Even when it is clear that spending cuts have to be made, we never tell a family which expenditures to cut or by how much, because the members of the family are the only ones who can decide which cuts can be made without inflicting severe damage on the atmosphere in the home. What we *do* advise families to do is to refrain from establishing a high standard of living in the first place, because once a family becomes accustomed to a certain standard of living, reducing that standard can be very painful, as you can unfortunately testify.

On the bright side, however, there are ways to minimize the pain of spending cuts and to turn the challenge of a reduced standard of living into an opportunity for achieving greater contentment.

To minimize the pain, we suggest that you and your husband – and possibly your children, depending on their ages and the family dynamics – sit down together and evaluate which items in your budget are the best candidates for elimination or reduction.

It's important to realize that the budget items that initially seem to be the most obvious places to cut are not always the best ones, because the absence of these items might be too glaring and painful. For example, if the lack of a second car means that your mobility is drastically curtailed and you feel miserable as a result, perhaps you would be better off keeping the car and feeding your kids scrambled eggs and peanut butter sandwiches for dinner. But if a menu of scrambled eggs and peanut butter sandwiches would lead to a revolt in your house, then by all means, get rid of the car and leave your menu alone.

The point is that even when budget cuts have to be made, they should be made in a way that causes your family the least pain. And what causes *your* family the least pain will be different from what causes another family the least pain. When deciding what to cut, you should consider only your family's needs, not anyone else's. It doesn't matter what anyone else considers important – what matters is that you retain the elements of your lifestyle that you and your family need in order to function well and maintain a pleasant atmosphere in your home.

After you have decided what budget items to cut and by how much, you can use some creativity to find ways to substitute for what is now missing in your lifestyle. Instead of canceling your trip to Switzerland entirely, for instance, you can take the family on a low-cost trip to a picturesque vacation area close to home. The destination is not what makes a vacation enjoyable – what makes a vacation enjoyable is the break in humdrum routine, the family togetherness, and the shared memories.

Minimizing the pain and finding creative budgetary alternatives should help reduce the anger and bitterness you feel. Along with that, you have to train yourself and your family to focus on the half of the cup that is full. You may not be able to afford music lessons, but you have food to eat, clothing to wear, and a roof above your heads. Your husband is making a decent living. Revel in the joy of living in a way that you can afford to live, of living off money that is *yours*.

Life does not have to be any less enjoyable on a tighter budget. Have you ever experienced the pleasure of finding an item you want marked down to half-price? Have you ever experienced the pleasure of making a simcha yourself, at home, instead of hosting a lavish, but impersonal, catered affair? Have you ever experienced the pleasure of scrimping and saving until you have enough money to buy something you really want? If not, now is your chance to discover these pleasures!

If in the past you enjoyed spending money freely, now you can learn to enjoy getting the most for your money. For many people – even rich people – getting a bargain is much more pleasurable than buying without looking at the price. Instead of feeling stifled by having to watch out for prices, look at it as a challenge – a *fun* challenge – to get what you need while remaining within your budget. It might take a conscious attitude shift on your part, but it is definitely possible for you to derive satisfaction from becoming an informed, savvy consumer.

It may also be a comfort to you to realize that your life has not really changed all that much. You had spending limitations before your husband's pay cut, and you were happy; you now have different spending limitations, and you can still be happy. The reason your previous spending limitations did not cause you distress was because you were so used to them, you were hardly even aware of them. When you went shopping, you instinctively gravitated towards items that were in your price range, without feeling deprived or bitter. But now that your spending limitations have narrowed, you are very conscious of them, and you are finding them difficult and restrictive. If you accept your new spending limitations, instead of chafing at them, you will find yourself once again gravitating painlessly to items that are in your new price range.

Beyond all the measures you can take to minimize the pain, there is another approach you can use to dispel any vestiges of deprivation and bitterness. This approach can be illustrated with the case of the man who came to a psychologist because he loved bunny rabbits. "I dream about bunny rabbits all the time," the man confessed. "Wherever I go I look for bunny rabbits."

This man's problem is not so unusual. Most of us do not have a particular affinity for bunny rabbits, but we do feel a pull towards things like fashionable clothing, upscale cars, jewelry, fine dining, home furnishings, leisure travel, and recreation. Like bunny rabbits, these things do have a place in the world. But a small place.

To give prominence to any type of material pursuit is to fill our world with bunny rabbits. How sad it is that so many people today are chasing bunny rabbit happiness! True happiness comes from giving, from growing, and from doing, not from getting, from buying, or from going.

Perhaps Hashem is taking away some of our bunny rabbits during this economic crisis to show us that there is more to life than bunny rabbits. If so, we should not look at these times as a crisis, but as an opportunity to reevaluate our values, priorities and goals and reshape our lifestyle to match those values, priorities and goals. For example, if family is our priority, doesn't it make sense to spend less time shopping and on-the-go and more time at home with the family? Or if our goal is to learn as much Torah as possible, then shouldn't we avoid the type of leisure activities that serve to distract us from Torah?

The fringe benefit of reshaping our lifestyles to match our true values, priorities and goals is that this usually translates into considerable financial savings – without causing anyone to feel deprived. That's because the things in life that are really important, the things that bring true contentment – *avodas Hashem*, relationships, health, accomplishment – do not have a price tag. And the happiness that comes from living in a way that is consistent with what we really want out of life is far more genuine form of happiness than the happiness that comes from having the things you want.

Not being able to afford the type of lifestyle you are accustomed to is unquestionably challenging, just like any other change. But instead of wallowing in the pain and feeling deprived and bitter, you can delight in the deep, lasting contentment and fulfillment that are yours for the taking.

STUDENT RESOURCE 15

CHILDREN'S NEEDS AND WANTS

Q: *I read your column about people who can afford luxuries but not sechar limud with interest. I am living within a budget that allows me to manage, but does not allow for major luxuries. Our apartment is useable, not beautiful; my clothes are from a gemach and so are the baby's. I can afford tutors for my children, though, and I make sure that my son's private rebbe is paid properly.*

I tell my children about needs and wants, and I attend to all of the former and a little of the latter. I teach the older ones to earn their own luxuries, and they babysit and deliver newsletters. But my children are ashamed of this attitude. For example, "everyone" in my thirteen-year-old daughter's class has a modern, expensive camera – and she doesn't.

Should I change my attitude due to my children's embarrassment? Am I giving them good chinuch, or just being stingy?

A: In our column about *sechar limud*, we talked about people who have money for luxuries but not for tuition. You are raising the opposite issue: people who have money for tuition and other objective priorities, but cannot afford to give their children luxuries.

It is clear that you have your spending priorities straight. The question, however, is whether your children are being impacted negatively by the spending priorities you have established.

Children and teenagers need to have the security of knowing that their parents will provide all of their needs. You obviously understand that, since you say that you attend to all of your children's needs and some of their wants.

But how are you determining what your children's needs and wants are? Often, the barometer of a child's needs is not necessarily what parents consider needs, but what the child's social environment has established as needs.

Needs are very subjective. In every community, there are different standards as to what children "need." Children, especially teenagers, crave to fit in with their peers. If all or most of your child's peers have a particular item, then your child might have a *need* for that item as well, even if you don't consider it at all necessary.

Obviously, you do not have to allow your children to be swept along with every fad, especially those that are not in keeping with your values. But if a child has a legitimate need, it is preferable to find a way to supply that need rather than tell the child, "We can't afford it."

If money is tight, then parents have to use some creativity in finding inexpensive, alternative ways to provide for their children's needs – for example, learning to sew, or buying at thrift shops.

It is not a good idea to make children earn money to pay for things they really need – even if the need is a subjective one. It is, however, legitimate to suggest that older children pay for, or at least chip in for, things they *want*.

With regard to the specific example you gave of "everyone" in your 13-year-old daughter's class having an expensive camera: you have to do your research and find out if "everyone" really means *everyone*. If, indeed, everyone (or just about everyone) in your daughter's class has a camera, then it is a need, and you should find a way to get it for her. If "everyone" means 20-30% of the class, however, then it is a want, not a need. That is where *chinuch* comes in: you, as a parent, have to decide if this situation calls for teaching your daughter budgetary restraint, or allowing her to use her own money, or indulging her.

How, you may ask, do we expect you to continue paying your children's tuition and private *rebbeim* if you have to supply your children with cameras and other whims? The answer is that as you become more tuned in to your children's individual needs, you will find that is possible to save money in ways you never thought of.

In the process of identifying needs, you will discover that that some of the things you thought were "needs" were not really needs at all. You will understand, for instance, that the child who needs the camera really has no need for the new school supplies you were planning to buy her, while her older sister needs a new wardrobe more than she needs the vitamin supplements you insist that she take.

If your children are expressing dissatisfaction and shame with the way you are providing for them, that is a warning sign that you might be depriving them of some of their needs. Deprivation is not *chinuch*; it actually teaches children to crave material possessions, accomplishing exactly the opposite of what *chinuch* is supposed to achieve.

The way to be *mechanech* children not to ascribe importance to material acquisition is by ensuring that material possessions do not become a focus, by virtue of either their presence or their absence. The less you turn money and possessions into issues, the more you will prepare your children for a life that emphasizes *ruchniyos*.

We at Mesila are staunch proponents of controlled consumption and *histapkus b'muat*, yet we strongly encourage families to create an atmosphere where money and frugality are not center stage. Words like "expensive" and "afford" should be used sparingly around children (and, for the sake of *shalom bayis*, between spouses, as well). Similarly, *histapkus b'muat* and *mesirus nefesh* for Torah are concepts that are not meant to be talked about, but practiced – happily.

By fostering an atmosphere of appreciation for Torah, *mitzvos* and *Yiddishkeit* in your home, you can subtly redirect your children's interests away from the many material enticements that the world has to offer, and in that way prevent many "needs" from arising. When children absorb a value system in which spiritual achievements are paramount, they are far less likely to feel deprived, even if their friends have more than they do.

As important as it is to supply children's material needs, it is even more important to provide them with the things that money cannot buy: attention, love, discipline, security and *mesorah*. If, despite your best efforts, you find that you simply do not have the means to supply all of your children's material needs, you should take comfort in the knowledge that you *can* supply your children with the things they need most.

Finding the right balance between exercising fiscal restraint and providing adequately for children can be challenging. For every family, the balance is different – and within every family, the balance shifts as the family dynamics change. As in all aspects of parenting, we need to seek guidance and daven for the *siyatta dishmaya* that will help us to meet our children's needs in the best possible way.

STUDENT RESOURCE 16

TAKING THE PAIN OUT OF BELT-TIGHTENING

Q: *I am choking financially, and I'm hoping that you can help me. I own a store in a large Jewish community, and my revenues have taken a nose-dive as a result of the economic crisis. During the good times, the store profits provided enough for my family to live on, but not much more. Now, however, it is not possible for us to live off the store's profits. I am hoping that business will pick up soon, but in the meantime, my family has had to make dramatic cuts to our standard of living. There does not seem to be anything left in our budget to cut, but even so, we are not managing to make ends meet, and we are falling into debt. Do you have any advice about how we can squeeze our budget further?*

A: In general, the way to cope with any type of financial difficulty is to look for ways to increase income and to decrease expenditures. From your description of your situation, it appears that the steps you have taken to deal with these difficult financial times have been primarily focused on decreasing your family's expenditures. Have you taken any steps to increase your income at the same time, whether by trying to boost the sales in your store or by finding other avenues of income? Have you and your wife brainstormed about ways to supplement the family's income during this recession?

First, Increase Income

The Mesila approach is to focus first on increasing income, then on decreasing expenditures, because increasing income has several advantages over decreasing expenditures.

First, increasing income is a positive, constructive step, while decreasing expenditures is a negative, restrictive step. As such, a family can more easily muster – and maintain – enthusiasm and motivation to increase its income than to decrease its expenditures. Second, encouraging people to increase their income involves no implied criticism of their lifestyle, while encouraging them to decrease their expenditures suggests that they are overspending or spending incorrectly. Third, the potential to increase income is unlimited – at least theoretically – while the potential to decrease expenditures is limited.

We would advise you to make sure that in your efforts to balance your budget, you are expending at least as much effort into increasing your income as into decreasing your expenditures. It is true that in today's economy, increasing income can be very difficult. But that is all the more reason to put effort into it.

Decreasing expenditures does have one important benefit over increasing income, however: it provides immediate, clearly

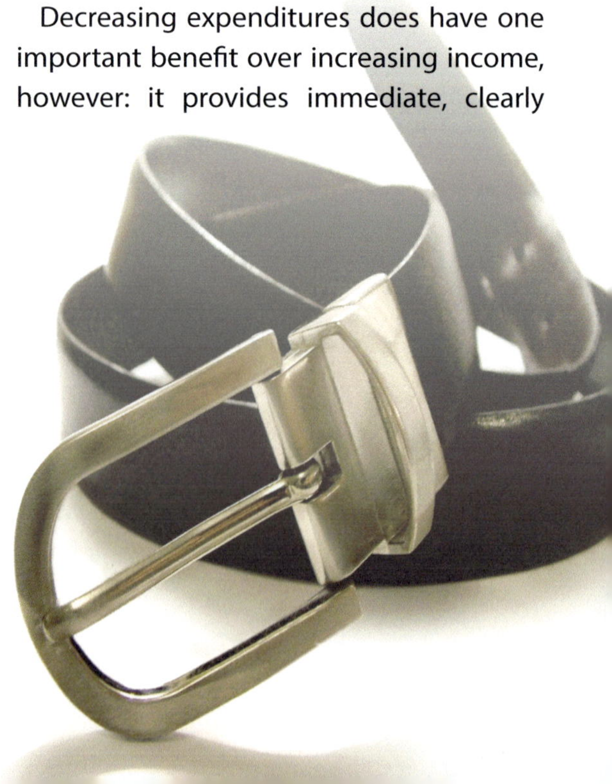

defined budgetary relief, while increasing income takes time and is not always predictable. Along with working to increase income, therefore, it is definitely important for you to look for ways to decrease your expenditures.

The Problem with Drastic Cuts

It is important to note that **the goal is not to drastically reduce expenditures** – even if you and your family are willing to do so – because that will squeeze you into a very tight budget, and Mesila has found that such drastic cuts rarely last. Instead, they create pressure and tension in the home and can cause you to despair and give up on balancing your budget.

Even minor spending cuts can result in tension between spouses and between parents and children. When people have to get used to living with less than they are accustomed to, it hurts, especially in the beginning. For that reason, we urge anyone who is trying to reduce spending to do it in a way that will cause the least pain to the family.

The approach that we recommend turns reducing expenditures into a positive exercise, rather than a negative one. In this approach, the goal is not to cut corners, trim the fat, or tighten your belt – the goal is to optimize your spending and build a brand new spending budget tailored to your family's needs. Instead of focusing on your past spending habits and seeing what you can cut, you will erase all of your spending history from your mind and come up with creative ways to meet your needs cost-effectively.

The way you have been spending money until now is definitely not the only way to meet your family's needs, and it is probably possible for you to meet those needs just as well – or better! – while spending less money. In fact, even if you would not have an urgent need to decrease your expenditures, it would be a good idea to periodically rethink your spending patterns and determine how you can get the most value for your money.

Building Your New Spending Plan

When you sit down to make a new spending plan, keep your mind open to all possibilities. Do not accept anything you have done until now as a given. What you have done in the past, and what your friends, relatives and neighbors are doing, is only marginally relevant during this exercise.

Your new spending plan should itemize all of your family's needs – from housing to dental work to keeping the children occupied during summer vacation. But it can involve major changes to the way you are meeting those needs. To illustrate: the housing market is down right now, so you may be able to renegotiate your rent or mortgage payments, or even move to a different house, at considerable savings. Your dentist might be an old friend whom you have been going to for years, but other dentists may do work that is equally good – at better prices. And you might not have to spend thousands of dollars to make summer vacation an enjoyable time for the whole family.

When building this new spending plan, do some research about the different options available to you, and don't be afraid to think out of the box. In addition, do not hesitate to switch any type of service provider, whether it's your phone company, your bank, or your insurance agent.

Plug the Leaks

Although you are erasing your old spending habits and building a spending plan from scratch, it is still important to examine your past and present spending patterns. These old spending patterns should not serve as a guide for building your new spending plan; they are important mainly for their research value.

Reviewing your spending will give you valuable information as to what your family's needs are, and will alert you to the many areas of your budget that you should reassess. It will also help you to see where money is leaking out unnecessarily.

You and your wife should track your expenditures for a period of two to three months. After that, you should prepare an itemized list, broken down into categories, in which you will tally how much you are spending on every item of your budget, from vitamins to haircuts to credit card fees. Then you will be able to evaluate which of these expenses can be eliminated or reduced. This exercise can save you a great deal of money, much of it painless.

Think Before You Spend

You will likely find that just the act of recording your expenditures results in significant savings. Having to write down what you are spending prods you to think before you spend, and thinking is one of the greatest money-saving tools available.

So much of the money we spend happens thoughtlessly – we buy a snack on the road when we could easily have taken one from the house, we pay late fees on bills that we simply forgot about, or we run to the hardware store to buy a tool when we have the identical tool sitting on a shelf in a storage room. By training ourselves to think before reaching into our wallets, we can bring ourselves significant budgetary relief.

Focus on Big-Ticket Items

When cutting expenses, people often focus on budgetary items that are relatively trivial ("No more candy! No more art lessons! Shut the lights!"), while overlooking the big-ticket items that comprise the lion's share of their budget. Things like rent or mortgage payments, insurance premiums, and car payments are huge expenses, and it is in those areas that spending cuts can provide the greatest financial relief.

At the same time, however, it is important to remember that every drop adds up, and every little bit that you save is significant. Your budget contains hundreds of small items, and when added up, these small items amount to a considerable percentage of your spending.

Another important aspect of streamlining your budget is ensuring that you are receiving any discounts, tax breaks and government benefits that you are entitled to. As a small business owner, you may be eligible for certain types of assistance, and we recommend that you speak to a competent accountant about this.

What Works for You

The challenge of decreasing expenditures is to streamline your budget without compromising the family's physical and emotional wellbeing. This challenge is highly individual, for one family might feel deprived living with something that another family is perfectly satisfied with. For instance, one family might have no problem buying generic or store-brand products – from detergent to breakfast cereal to clothing – while another family might find it very difficult to abandon the brand names it is accustomed to. Which family is right? It's not a question of right and wrong. It's a question of what works.

If you are willing to think creatively and reprogram your family's spending habits, you may be pleasantly surprised to find that your budget can go a lot further than you thought.

STUDENT RESOURCE 17

BEFORE YOU THROW IN THE TOWEL ON BUDGETING

Q: *My family would probably be described as a typical middle-class family. Our income is decent, but not great, and our expenses are close at the heels of our income – too close for comfort, probably, but no worse than most other families. Our home is not in danger of foreclosure, so we can't be doing that badly, considering the crisis.*

I've been following your column for some time now and I've actually tried implementing much of your advice. I tried sitting down with my wife and building a budget plan, but it was a dismal failure. We decided to record all of our expenditures so we could see where our money was going, but we just could not remember to write everything down, so that attempt petered out after a few days. The first month of our new budget plan, we ended up spending so much more than we had planned and buying so many things that weren't included in the budget that we just gave up on budgeting. We also tried starting to put aside money for savings – and this something we both really wanted to do – but when our washing machine broke suddenly it wiped out all of our newfound savings and we just couldn't manage to get the savings habit started again.

No matter how many times I try to manage my finances the way I would like to, I always find myself falling back into the same old patterns, the same old problems, time after time. I was about to resign myself either to the fact that I am not cut out for budgeting, or to the fact that I just don't have enough time to be busy with it, but before I threw in the towel on budgeting I thought I'd ask you why I'm having such a hard time with this.

A: Your question is one that we are sure everyone can relate to on some level. Financial management can be very frustrating, and it can be very tempting to let go of the financial steering wheel and allow your finances to coast along on their own. The problem is that the path to financial stability is strewn with hazards, and navigating that path on cruise control can lead you into a tailspin of debt, dependency and unbearable stress.

Financial management today is a complex, bewildering task, one that requires a combination of strategic planning, self-discipline and persistence. For some very disciplined people, financial management comes easily, but for most people, it is a difficult and frustrating task. That's why even bright, capable people like you feel they are "not cut out" for budgeting.

Financial management wasn't always as hard as it is today. In the not too distant past, money was something you carried in your wallet or kept under the floorboards. If you wanted to buy something – and there wasn't that much to buy – you took out a few coins or bills and never had to think later about how to pay for it. If you didn't have the money to buy what you wanted, you either did without or scrimped and saved until you had the money for it.

Back then, money was something tangible, not a bunch of abstract numbers on a bank statement. Budgeting was a straightforward task: you counted your money, and then allocated it for the things you needed the most. You also tried to put something aside for a rainy day, so that you would not have to go hungry if your source of income dried up.

Many people ask us why there is a need for an organization like Mesila nowadays, since "Our grandparents managed just fine without Mesila." Indeed, our grandparents did not need Mesila – they had Mesila in their bones, and living without a *cheshbon* was unthinkable to them. They also were not under continuous bombardment by a multibillion-dollar advertising industry hawking the wares of the global marketplace and modern technology, nor were they at the mercy of banks and credit card companies offering "attractive financing options" to pay for all that the 21st century has to offer.

Mesila started out eleven years ago as an organization that helped people in Israel who were in debt and could not get their finances under control. But in the process of helping hundreds of families and businesses work towards financial stability, we realized that financial management difficulties transcend geographic and socioeconomic divides, and almost everyone today needs help managing their finances. That was why three years ago we shifted our focus to education and prevention, instead of crisis intervention.

The economic crisis we are now experiencing is the result of poor financial management at every level, from corporate bigwigs all the way down to the little guy with the big mortgage. We believe that the answer to this crisis is not dramatic government bailouts, but old-fashioned self-discipline and careful budgeting.

Thankfully, you are still a step ahead of the crisis. But that is much too close for comfort. You are lucky that you had some savings to tide you past a broken washing machine, but what would happen if your boiler went? We are not trying to be pessimistic, but we think that burying your head in the sand and hoping that things will work out is not optimism, but poor planning. You need to be aware of what is going on with your finances, you need to establish financial goals for the future, and you need to create and follow a budget that will help you realize these goals. The other option is financial mayhem, which in the worst-case scenario leads to disaster, and in the best-case scenario leads to putting out fires.

What does "putting out fires" mean? It means discovering all of a sudden that your bank account is overdrawn and having to face all the people to whom you wrote bounced checks. It means paying 20% interest on your credit card balance until you come up with "extra" money (we've never actually heard anyone say they have extra money) to pay it off. It means waking up in middle of the night and remembering that you don't have the money your daughter needs in the morning to pay for her school trip. And it means living a life of balance transfers and debt juggling, borrowing money from one source to repay a loan from a different source.

If correct financial management is difficult and time-consuming, poor financial management is infinitely more difficult and time-consuming. The difference is that correct financial management requires you to exert yourself and exercise self-discipline ahead of time, while poor financial management allows you to take the path of least resistance and suffer the consequences later. Although this path is ultimately the harsher one, it is the default route and therefore the one more trodden.

Like you, many people tell us that they don't have time to create, follow and review their budget plans on a regular basis. That's a bit like saying that you don't have time to look both ways before you cross the street. If you think that analogy is exaggerated, that is because you haven't spent as many hours as we have helping families to extricate themselves from financial crises that could have been avoided.

We don't want you to become one of those families, and that's why we are trying to help you understand that correct financial management is not just a nice bonus; it's a necessity. The investment of time and effort now to create and follow a budget can spare you a tremendous amount of time and frantic effort later to come up with money to pay for sudden (or not-so-sudden) expenses.

Besides for preventing financial difficulties in the future, correct financial management has tremendous positive benefits. Having your finances under control will reduce the amount of financial tension in your life, which will in turn make you a more relaxed person and therefore a better husband and father. If your finances are being managed correctly, you will have an easier time concentrating during your davening and Torah learning, and you will be free to pursue your livelihood to the best of your ability without feeling like a slave to your *parnassah* worries.

Living with a budget is emancipating, for it allows you to truly enjoy everything Hashem gives you without having to worry about whether you can afford it. Although it may require you to give up certain comforts or conveniences, living with a budget will bring you peace of mind and security, which will make every moment of your life sweeter. Shlomo Hamelech says as much when he tells us that a piece of dry piece of bread that has peace in it is better than a banquet where tension and strife reign (*Mishlei* 17:1)

Correct financial management compels you to look inward and make decisions based on what *you* need, what *you* can afford, and what is important to *you*, instead of looking outward at what the neighbors have and wondering how they can afford it. Focusing on your neighbor's Lexus will never bring you any happiness, but focusing on what *you* really want out of life will. By forcing you to clearly define your priorities and goals, a budget can help you to manage your money in the way that will bring you the maximum satisfaction out of life.

Understanding the benefits of correct

financial management is the best way to motivate yourself to muster the self-discipline and persistence to track your expenditures, stick to your budget plan, and save for the future. Your wife also has to be convinced of the benefits of correct financial management, since the slightest resistance on her part can torpedo your efforts.

Once both of you are convinced of the benefits, the next step is to develop a system of financial management that works for you. You might have to experiment with a few different approaches, but if you persist, we are sure that you can find the approach that is right for you.

Here are some practical suggestions for coping with the specific issues you mentioned:

- To track you expenditures successfully, keep a small notebook with you at all times to record expenditures as they happen, and save all of your receipts, bills and bank statements.

- To ensure that you stick to your budget, schedule specific times when you and your wife can sit down alone to review your budget and make any necessary changes. You and your wife are teammates, not adversaries, and your "budget meetings" should be calm, pleasant discussions. These meetings are the time for you and your wife to communicate any concerns you may have and to look for ways to address those concerns. Decisions made at each of these budget meetings should be written down, since writing down budgetary information contributes to financial control and discipline.

- To strengthen your resolve, you can read Mesila's articles and other materials, use our budget questionnaires, or attend a Mesila financial management workshop. (If you wish to organize a workshop series in your community, please contact us and we will try to arrange it.) Being part of the Mesila movement can turn financial management into a rewarding experience, instead of a pain in the neck, and can give you the tools and enthusiasm to take control of your finances in a lasting way.

52

STUDENT RESOURCE 18

SEMINARY BUDGET

Income

Weekly (average): ______

Yearly (birthday, Chanuka, etc.): ______

Other: ______

Monthly expenditures

Food	
Grocery food	
Fruit and veggies	
Paper goods	
Meals outside school	
Drinks	
Ice coffee and ice cream	
Pizza pie	
Other	
Total:	

Transportation	
Buses	
Cabs	
Trains	
Total:	

Communications	
Cell phone to cell phone calls	
Cell phone to land line calls	
Long distance calls	
DSL fees	
Other	
Total:	

Health and personal care	
Medical insurance	
Medications	
Toiletries	
Fitness	
Other	
Total:	

Miscellaneous	
Tzedakah	
Laundry	
Shabbos gift	
Other	
Total:	

Yearly expenditures

Sefarim & text books	
Extra fees to school	
Heater or fan	
School supplies (initial shopping)	
Rosh Hashanah and Yom Kippur seats	
Mishloach Manos	
Matza and wine for Pesach	
Gifts for going home	
Cab to go to airport for departure flight	
Lost cell-phone pieces at end of year	
Other	
Total:	

Vacations	
Succos vacation	
Mid-winter vacation	
Pesach vacation	

Fluctuating expenses

Clothing	
School supplies (replenishment)	
Long distance travel	
Gifts for friends	
Other	

Unit 3

Consumerism and Credit

Introduction

When people in a society shop and spend money, it is a sign of a healthy economy. But though increased consumption may be good for the economy, is it good for you? Years ago, people used to shop when they experienced a lack and had the money with which to buy what they needed. Nowadays, business and advertising create needs where there were none, and easy credit leads people to buy items that they cannot afford. Shopping has morphed from "just another chore" to a very costly form of recreation and a way of filling emotional voids.

The natural outcome of uncalculated spending is a rapid build-up of debt. Hidden debts, such as bank overdraft and credit debt, are often not felt until they have reached monstrous proportions, and these debts can be devastating both for household finances and Shalom Bayis.

In addition to the financial pitfalls of unbridled spending, the shopping trend has affected our mindset as well, creating a more materialistic and competitive society. But we can learn to shop smart and use means of payment wisely, so as to harness consumerism for our benefit and not be reeled into unnecessary credit debt.

Goals

- To recognize the value of consumerism, from the Torah outlook
- To learn how to resist pressures to create needs where there are none
- To identify an overspending tendency - shopaholism - and deal with it
- To differentiate between means of payment and identify the pros and cons of each
- To learn how to use credit to the consumer's benefit, without falling into its traps
- To understand the Torah view on loans and recognize the "hidden loans," such as credit card debt
- To differentiate between positive loans (such as mortgages) and negative loans (to cover running expenses)
- To apply smart shopping habits to mortgage negotiation
- To learn how to manage existing debts effectively

STUDENT RESOURCE 19

TORAH VIEW ON THE ECONOMY

במדבר רבא כב, ז

ולמה נקרא שמם **זוזין**? שזזים מזה ונותנין לזה

Why is [money] called "zuzin"? Because it moves ["zaz"] from one and is given to another. (Bamidbar Rabbah 22:7)

מסכת ברכות ג:

נכנסו חכמי ישראל אצלו, אמרו לו: אדונינו המלך, עמך ישראל צריכין פרנסה.

אמר להם: לכו והתפרנסו זה מזה.

The Sages of Israel came to [Dovid Hamelech] and said to him, "Our master, the king, your nation Israel needs sustenance!" He said to them, "Go and earn a living from one another." (Berachos 3b)

STUDENT RESOURCE 20

DR. SEUSS ON Consumerism

Consumerism is based on creating needs where none existed before.

In **The Lorax**, by Dr. Seuss, a fellow opens a factory for a new type of garment called a "Thneed," and a creature named the Lorax ridicules him for creating this useless item. To which the fellow responds:

"A Thneed's a fine something that all people need!
It's a shirt. It's a sock. It's a glove. It's a hat.
But it has other uses. Yes, far beyond that.
You can use it for carpets. For pillows! For sheets!
Or curtains! Or covers for bicycle seats!"

The Lorax said, "Sir! You are crazy with greed.
There is no one on earth
who would buy that fool Thneed!"
But the very next minute I proved he was wrong.
For, just at that minute, a chap came along,
and he thought that the Thneed I had knitted was great.
He happily bought it for three ninety-eight.

I laughed at the Lorax, "You poor stupid guy!
You never can tell what some people will buy."

STUDENT RESOURCE 21

AM I A SHOPAHOLIC?

Question: *Shopping has been my favorite pastime ever since I've been a teenager. I love to buy things – groceries, clothing, household items, you name it. I often find myself heading out to a store in the evenings when I have nothing else to do. I've noticed a pattern in which I'll go into a store on the spur of the moment and buy a few things, only to go back to that store a few days later to return some items, at which point I'll inevitably find something else to purchase. My family members and friends comment about my spending habits, calling me a "shopaholic" and telling me that I spend too much. How do I know if I really have a spending problem? And if I do have a spending problem, how can I overcome it?*

A: Not knowing the details of your lifestyle and spending habits, we cannot tell you whether you have a spending problem. But we can tell you that your willingness to confront the issue is a very good first step in overcoming your spending problem, if indeed you have one.

When does spending become a problem? Any type of behavior or characteristic taken to an extreme is problematic, and spending is no different. The Rambam teaches us that the middle road is the golden path, and the ability to strike a balance between the two extremes in every middah is the hallmark of healthy behavior.

Spending problems come in two varieties – stinginess and extravagance, representing the two polar extremes of the spending spectrum. Our goal is to find a middle road that allows us to spend enough to meet our needs and obligations, but not so much that we squander money needlessly.

The terms "stinginess" and "extravagance" are quite subjective, because the size of a person's budget is a major factor in determining whether the person spends too much or too little. But how much money a person has is by no means the only factor in determining whether he or she has a spending problem. Spending problems are as a much a behavioral issue as a financial issue. There are poor people who are miserly, and there are rich people who are miserly. There are poor people who overspend, and there are rich people who overspend.

The sign of a stinginess problem is when a person has difficulty spending money on items that he and his family clearly require – not because he doesn't have the money, but because he cannot bring himself to spend it. This creates an atmosphere of deprivation and penny-

Reprinted from *Your Money and Your Life: Mesila's Down-to-Earth, Torah-Based Strategies for Managing Your Finances*, by M. Heimowitz

pinching in the home, which is often accompanied by a fixation with money and prices.

When does overspending become a problem? For every person, the line between healthy spending and overspending will be drawn in a different place, but we can identify four general parameters that can help you to determine whether you are overspending.

1. **You spend more than you can afford.** There are three ways to assess whether you are spending more than you can afford. One, if you consistently spend more than you earn, and you either accumulate debt or eat away at your savings as a result. Two, if your income is reasonable but you are nevertheless unable to put aside any money for the future. And three, if you spend money on luxury or non-essential items and you are then unable to pay for basic or essential items.

2. **You spend money to fill an emotional void.** While shopping can be a pleasurable experience and can provide some measure of stress relief, it should not be used consistently as an outlet for negative feelings such as sadness, inadequacy, boredom, guilt, fear, anger, or nervousness. Spending money is not a healthy response to negative feelings, because the act of swiping a credit card and walking away with a shopping bag does nothing to dispel the source of those feelings. Any feeling of emotional relief that shopping provides is therefore short-lived and superficial.

3. **You buy things that you do not need and never use.** If your closet is full of items that still have price tags, if you often wonder what possessed you to buy a particular item that you have no use for, or if you frequently make excuses for – or worse, lie about – your purchases and how much they cost, then it is likely that your spending is problematic.

4. **Your spending is adversely affecting other areas of your life.** Even if you and your family are not suffering financially because of your spending habits, your spending might be harmful to you or to your loved ones in other ways. Do you have frequent arguments with your family members about your spending habits? Are your children being neglected because you are out shopping too much? Has your marriage been reduced to a collection of shared things, instead of shared goals and shared communication? Does your life revolve around material acquisition, to the point that you are desensitized to the pleasures of spirituality and meaningful relationships?

Severe Overspending

In extreme cases, people can actually develop an addiction to shopping – known scientifically as oniomania, or colloquially as "shopaholism" – if they get used to spending money in order to squelch negative feelings. These people might buy ten items when they really need only one, or they might pay outrageous amounts of money for things they have little or no use for.

Shopping addicts experience a rush of endorphins when they spend money, which gives them a brief but exhilarating escape from life's painful realities. As soon as that feeling of euphoria subsides, they begin to crave the pleasurable sensation they associate with shopping, and they feel an uncontrollable urge to spend money again. Between spending episodes, shopping addicts are typically plagued by anxiety, shame, and guilt, and think about money excessively. This cycle is typical of addictive behavior, and professional intervention is usually required in order to break the cycle.

Overcoming the Problem

If your spending has reached out-of-control proportions, to the point where it can be classified as compulsive or addictive, then you will need to seek professional help. But if you still have some measure of control over your spending, we will offer several suggestions for reining it in to a point where it is no longer problematic.

› Don't carry your wallet with you when you don't need it. If you don't have money or a credit card with you, then you will have to come back later if you want to buy an item that you see. This is a good way to test whether you really need or want the item, and can help to reduce impulse purchases.

› Get rid of your credit cards. When used properly, credit cards can be a very convenient and useful tool. But if you have a tendency to overspend, you should avoid credit cards completely. Credit cards make it dangerously easy to spend money, since they eliminate the pain you experience when you have to part with your money. The pain of parting with money is actually a healthy pain, because it ensures that you item you are spending money on justifies the pain involved.

› Shop when you are not sad, stressed, excited, or in a rush. People tend to spend more, and buy things they don't need, when they are feeling down, or when they are under pressure. People who are very happy, excited, or on an emotional high also tend to spend more. And the less time people have, the more money they tend to spend.

› Avoid temptation. Stay away from the stores you tend to spend money in. If you have a particular friend who spends a lot, don't go shopping with her.

› Develop constructive emotional outlets. There are many constructive ways to relieve negative feelings, but spending money is not one of them. If you are feeling down, talk to a friend, pick up a Tehillim, or go for a walk, instead of heading instinctively for the mall. Keep in mind that "retail therapy" is therapeutic for retailers, not for customers.

› Find alternative recreational activities. You don't have to buy anything in order to have a good time. Instead of associating shopping with leisure and relaxation, condition yourself to see shopping primarily as a functional and task-oriented activity, and plan leisure activities that do not involve any purchases.

› Learn to express love and gratitude in non-tangible ways. People who enjoy buying things often ascribe disproportionate value or importance to tangible objects and resort to gift-giving in order to express love and gratitude. But emotions like these are best expressed in words, whether spoken or written. Tangible gifts should be reserved for special occasions; otherwise, they lose their value in the eye of the recipient. Even when you do decide to buy a gift, remember that a gift is only as meaningful as the sentiment underlying it, and the amount of money you spend on a gift does not determine its value.

- Build a budget that includes an allowance for discretionary spending. If you tend to overspend, then it is doubly important for you to have a clearly defined budget that governs the amount you spend on variable expenditures such as food, clothing, gifts, and household items. But in order for you to succeed in sticking to your budget, it is also important that you give yourself some breathing room and allocate some money towards non-essential or impulse purchases. This way, you will not feel stifled by your budget and you will not be tempted to abandon it any time you succumb to the temptation to buy something that is not absolutely necessary. To make sure that you remain accountable to your budget, you should build it together with your spouse or a close friend or relative, and review it together with that person on a regular basis.

Questionnaire

?"Am I a "Shopaholic

1) **Is shopping your primary pastime and entertainment?**

   No (0)

   Sometimes (5)

   Definitely (10)

2) **Do you have interests or hobbies outside of shopping?**

   Tons of other interests (0)

   Some (5)

   No (10)

3) **Do you find that shopping steadies your nerves when you are stressed?**

   I don't see the connection (0)

   Sometimes (5)

   Works like a charm every time (10)

4) **Do you think about sales, stores and shopping centers even when there is nothing you need?**

   How sad (0)

   Here and there (5)

   For sure! (10)

5) **Do you have a fear of missing out of things when you're not up to date on sales or haven't shopped for a while?**

   Not at all (0)

   Occasionally (5)

   How did you know that? (10)

6) Are you surprised at how much you've spent once you left the store?

Sometimes (0)

Often (5)

Always (10)

7) Lets say you come to the checkout counter and you realize you took too many things... Do you - - -

Quickly run and put it back (0)

Realize: "Oh, wait - some of this might be useful in the end" (5)

Just get it - you know you won't be sorry (10)

8) Do you work with an organized list when you shop?

Of course - how else can I keep track of what I need? (0)

Who has time? I think it through and try to remember (5)

Sure - a list of stores with sales and closeouts (10)

9) Does your family think you have an extreme or extravagant spending habit?

No (0)

Just my brother (5)

They make constant fun of me (10)

10) Money in my pocket gives me a feeling of...

Nothing at all (0)

Security and comfort: now I'll be okay (5)

Exhilaration: let's go! (10)

11) Do you express warmth or closeness through a gift?

At times, accompanied by a warm note (0)

Often (5)

Always - that's how I show affection (10)

12) If you can't give a tangible gift when you want to, for whatever reason, how anxious or embarrassed do you feel?

If I can, I can, and if I can't, I can't (0)

If it's an occasion when most people give I feel uncomfortable (5)

I'm mortified if I can't give in a super perfect way (10)

13) If you feel lonely or spiritually empty, do you shop rather than deal with the core issue?

Not at all (0)

Sometimes but it doesn't really do the trick (5)

Shopping makes it all go away (10)

14) If you walk down the street holding lots of bags from shopping, you feel...

Like your hands hurt (0)

Successful - I accomplished! (5)

Totally empowered and on top of the world (10)

15) How many times a month do you shop?

1-3 times (0)

3-5 times (5)

5-31 times (10)

16) Are you easily swayed by advertisement and readily believe what advertisers tell you?

No (0) Maybe (5) Yes (10)

STUDENT RESOURCE 22

MEANS OF PAYMENT

CASH

PROS

- People know whether they have money to spend.
- The money is tangible, not an abstract number on a bank or credit card statement. This creates greater psychological resistance to parting with it, and leads people to think more about spending it.
- From the standpoint of financial responsibility and restraint, many of the disadvantages of cash are actually advantages.

CONS

- People often don't have cash readily available, and obtaining cash can be a hassle.
- Obtaining cash may involve bank fees.
- There is no recourse in the event of loss or theft.
- Once payment is made, the money cannot be retrieved. (Unlike a check or credit card payment that can be stopped.)
- Payment has to be made in person; it cannot be made by telephone, by mail or online.
- Cash transactions are difficult to track or keep records of.
- Possibility of counterfeit bills.

CHECK

PROS

- Payment can be made by mail.
- Can be used when there is no cash available.
- Can be post-dated to delay payment.
- Can be stopped in the event of loss, theft, or a payment dispute.
- Convenient as a deposit on a purchase or as a form of guarantee.
- Payment can be made in advance, on any date in the future.

CONS

- Check payments are difficult to track because it is uncertain when the checks will be deposited.
- When more than one person is writing checks on an account, it can lead to chaos.
- Bounced checks, or checks that have mistakes or other technical problems can lead to inconvenience, embarrassment and hefty charges.
- Possibility of fraud.
- Ease of delaying payment may cause people to go into debt.

CREDIT CARD

PROS

- Convenient and available.
- Insurance against theft.
- Easy to cancel in the event of loss.
- Payment can be made by telephone or online.
- Can be used anywhere in the world.
- Can be used by all members of the family.
- Easy to track.
- Credit limits make it impossible to spend more than a certain amount.
- Payment can be made in installments.
- Earn air miles and rewards.

CONS

- People spend more (30% more, studies show) because it is convenient and because they do not feel the pain of parting with their money.
- Multiple credit cards can lead to chaos.
- Paying in installments can lead to exceeding budget-ary limits.
- Credit option can be halachically problematic.
- Credit cards deceive people into thinking that they have money when they really do not.
- Incurs high interest if paid late.

STUDENT RESOURCE 23

CLIMBING THE MOUNTAIN OF CREDIT CARD DEBT

Question: *I know that Mesila is against using credit cards, but I have found that it is difficult for me to keep the right amounts of cash on hand, and I often resort to using my credit card. As a result, I've built up a bit of a balance on my credit card – or cards, I should say – and I'm wondering if you have any advice how I can pay it off.*

A: Mesila is not, in principle, opposed to credit cards, nor do we consider cash the preferred payment method in all situations. One of Mesila's guiding principles is to promote financial management principles and attitudes that are universally relevant, while avoiding specific tips and suggestions. So rather than issuing a blanket statement regarding whether you should be using credit cards or not, we will share several general guidelines that should help you decide for yourself.

Credit cards can be a very useful and convenient tool, when used correctly. The trouble is that many people misuse their credit cards by charging more than they can afford each month. Credit card companies actually *rely* on people misusing their cards; in fact, interest charged on outstanding balances represents the primary way in which credit card companies generate revenue. In 2007, people in the U.S. who carried a monthly balance paid $18.1 billion in penalty fees. With annual earnings of about $30 billion, the credit card industry is the most profitable one in the United States.

There are many advantages to using credit cards. You never run of out money. You are generally insured against theft, and you can easily cancel the card if you lose it. In contrast, cash that is lost or stolen is usually gone forever. You can use your credit card to pay for purchases by telephone or online, rather than mailing a check or paying by cash in person. Most credit cards can be used anywhere in the world, regardless of the local currency, and you can order cards for all of your family members. Depending on the card issuer's policy, purchases made using the card may be protected against theft, loss, or accidental damage that occurs within a certain period of time.

Credit card statements make it relatively straightforward to track your purchases on a monthly basis and keep a record of how your money is being spent. Cash, on the other hand, has no paper trail, and it is difficult to remember exactly where the money in your wallet went.

We will point out that all of these advantages are available through bank or debit cards as well, although purchase protection may not be offered on certain debit cards. The big difference, however, is that these cards draw on money that is already in your bank account, rather than creating a de facto debt that has to be paid at the end of the billing cycle. The only feature that credit cards offer that debit cards do not usually have is the possibility of earning rewards, in the form of airline miles, cash-back offers, or other perks.

So much for the advantages of using credit cards. Now let's talk about the drawbacks. Drawback number one is that they make it deceptively easy to spend money, whether you have the money or you don't. The act of swiping a credit card is not nearly as painful as taking actual money out of your wallet, and the psychological deterrent to parting with your money is therefore lessened considerably when paying with a credit card. Studies show that people spend about 30% more when paying by credit card than when paying with cash, and we think it is fair to assume that the extra 30% is money that could have been put to better use.

The other major drawback of credit cards is that they are a form of loan. When you take a loan, you borrow money and commit to repaying it at a later date. When you use a credit card, you also borrow money – but without realizing it. Mesila's philosophy is that a loan in which you realize that you are borrowing money is preferable to a loan in which you do not realize that you are borrowing money, simply because you are less likely to borrow, and more likely to repay, when the decision to take the loan was a conscious one.

Credit card debt is one of the worst forms of debt, for two reasons. One, it usually carries very high interest rates. Two, there is no repayment deadline for the debt. As long as you keep making minimum payments, credit card companies are quite happy to keep tacking interest onto your balance and let your debt swell to ever-greater proportions. Unpleasant as it may be to have creditors breathing down your back, it is a far healthier situation when a debt is collected at the end of its term than when a debt is allowed to balloon endlessly.

Not only do credit cards charge high interest rates, but there is very little limit as to how much they can raise your rate. Credit card companies are legally allowed to monitor your credit report, and should you make a late payment on a loan, a different credit card, or a utility bill, your interest rates can be increased dramatically, even if you have never missed a payment on that particular card. There are a number of other reasons you may see your rates spike. These include bouncing a check, exceeding your credit limit, having too much debt or credit, getting a new credit card, and applying for an auto loan or mortgage.

Because credit card debt is so dangerous, our advice is that the only people who should use credit cards are those who (a) can rein in their spending despite the painless convenience of plastic and (b) pay their balance in full every month consistently. People who swipe their cards without giving it the same thought that they would when spending cash should rather spend cash, unless they are paying for something that they cannot possibly be spending more for by using a credit card (dental work, for instance, or a utility bill). And people who carry over a balance on their credit cards, even occasionally, should probably avoid using credit cards completely.

If you are able to use a credit card correctly, there are a few things we recommend:

› *Choose the right card.*

Make sure that your card provides a grace period of at least 20 days from the date of purchase until payment is due. Without a grace period, you'll be charged interest before you even get your bill. There are cards that offer airline miles, cash back on purchases, and points for rewards programs, and if you are using a credit card, you might as well get something in return. However, if there is an annual fee associated with your rewards card, make sure the benefits outweigh the cost.

› *Don't have too many cards.*

Keeping track of even one credit card can be quite a challenge. When keeping track of two or more cards, mistakes (such as missed payments or forgetting to cancel the card before annual fees kick in) are more likely to go by unnoticed. Unless you have a very good reason for keeping a second or third credit card, get rid of it.

But what if you have already fallen into credit card debt? Here are some suggestions for climbing out of the morass.

› *Ask for clemency.*

If you missed only one payment, you can call your credit card company and ask them to waive interest and late fees. Credit card companies will waive these fees on occasion, if you generally pay on time.

› *Stop using your credit cards.*

If you're already behind on your monthly payments, don't aggravate the situation by accumulating more credit card debt. Although this may seem obvious, it is actually the opposite of how people generally work. The tendency is that once people owe money, they lose a major psychological deterrent towards borrowing, and they let their debt slowly inflate. ("What's the difference if I owe $600 or $900?" "If I already owe $60,000, another $5,000 won't make any difference.") Cut your losses *now*, and don't allow yourself to charge even one additional item.

› *Take out a loan to pay off your credit card debt.*

Almost any type of loan is preferable to credit card debt because interest rates are generally much lower and there is a specific repayment timeframe. With a loan, you can work out repayment terms that reflect your ability to repay, which helps you discipline yourself to put aside a fixed sum every month for debt repayment. With credit card debt, there is no such discipline, since there is no obligation to repay anything more than the minimum payment.

› *Do a balance transfer to another card.*

While you will pay a fee, transferring your outstanding balance to a card with a lower interest rate will decrease the amount you carry from month to month. By doing a balance transfer instead of allowing interest fees to build up, you give yourself some breathing room to pay off your debt. But beware – this is a very stopgap measure. You can't keep doing balance transfers for very long since there are only so many transfers credit card companies will allow you to do, and besides, multiple balance transfers will cause your finances to become chaotic.

› *Find a card with a low interest rate.*

Some credit cards offer relatively low interest rates. Shopping around for a better rate than the one you currently have can save you hundreds or even thousands of dollars a month (that is, if your credit rating is good enough for you to be eligible for these offers). Look out, however, for introductory offers that end after several months or exclusions that limit the low rate to new purchases only.

› *Negotiate a better interest rate.*

You might have to spend a long time on the phone with your credit card company, but it's worth it to get your interest rate reduced by even a few points. If possible, ask your company to match another company's offer. If your company is unwilling to cooperate, you can mention that you may be forced to declare personal bankruptcy, if that is really an option. This gets the companies scared, because they are the ones who stand to lose from a bankruptcy.

› *Never, ever miss a minimum payment.*

Missing minimum payments is a big no-no, and can severely damage your credit rating. Having a good credit rating is important, because many types of creditors besides credit card companies – including utilities, hospitals, landlords, insurance companies, and banks – can report delinquent payments to credit bureaus, as well as access your credit history. Since credit card companies are among those monitoring and contributing to customers' credit reports, a late or missed payment on one charge account could cause your rates and fees to increase on a completely separate account – even your car insurance premiums.

Pay off credit card balances from smallest to largest.

The smallest debts are the easiest to pay off, and clearing them out of the way helps you make the fastest progress towards getting your finances in order. The fewer debts you have to pay back, the easier it will be to see the light at the end of the tunnel, and the more motivated you will be to tackle the larger, scarier debts.

› *Make micro-payments.*

In addition to the minimum payments, send in whatever small amounts you can to gradually pay off your balance.

› *Get professional debt counseling assistance.*

Climbing a mountain of credit card debt can be a very tough task to tackle alone. If there is a Mesila branch in your community, we encourage you to apply for our family counseling program. If there is no Mesila branch in your community, seek the guidance of a qualified debt counselor.

STUDENT RESOURCE 24

STUDENT RESOURCE 24

TORAH VIEW ON LOANS

ברכת המזון

ונא אל תצריכנו לא לידי מתנת בשר ודם ולא לידי הלוואתם

Please do not make us needy of the gifts of human hands nor of their loans.

פרשת כי תבוא

"יִפְתַּח ה' לְךָ אֶת אוֹצָרוֹ הַטּוֹב אֶת הַשָּׁמַיִם לָתֵת מְטַר אַרְצְךָ בְּעִתּוֹ וּלְבָרֵךְ אֵת כָּל מַעֲשֵׂה יָדֶךָ וְהִלְוִיתָ גּוֹיִם רַבִּים וְאַתָּה לֹא תִלְוֶה".

Hashem will open for you His treasure-house of goodness, the heavens, to give the rain of your loand in its time and to bless all your handiwork and you will lend to many nations and you will not borrow". (Devarim 28:12)

פרשת כי תבוא

הוּא יַלְוְךָ וְאַתָּה לֹא תַלְוֶנּוּ

He will lend to you and you will not lend to him.

קובץ אגרות חזון איש

...לשלוח יד בהלוואות, המשחית את אצילות הנפש, וגורם בושה לעצמך ולאחרים.

...To extend your hand for loans, which destroy the soul's nobility, and cause shame to yourself and to others. (Kovetz Igros of Chazon Ish, 2nd volume)

שמות רבא לא,ו

נשך - רבית שהוא כנשיכת נחש שנושך חבורה קטנה ברגלו ואינו מרגיש ופתאום הוא מבצבץ ונופח עד קדקדו כך רבית אינו מרגיש ואינו ניכר עד שהרבית עולה ומחסרו ממון הרבה.

Interest - which the Torah calls neshech, similar to the Hebrew word for "bite," neshichah - is like a snakebite. When a snake bites, it creates a small wound in a person's leg, which he does not sense, but suddenly, it puffs up and swells until his head. Similarly, a person does not notice interest until it grows and costs him a great deal of money. (Shemos Rabbah 31:6)

במדבר רבא יח, יב

ארבעה נקראו רשעים... והלווה ואינו משלם שנאמר (תהלים לז) לוה רשע ולא ישלם וצדיק חונן ונותן.

Four people are called "evildoers"...and one who borrows and does not repay, as it says (Tehillim 37), An evildoer borrows and does not repay, while a righteous person is gracious and gives. (Bamidbar Rabbah 18:12)

אסור ללוה לקחת הלואה ולהוציאה שלא לצורך ולאבדה עד שלא ימצא המלוה ממה לגבות חובו ואם עושה כן נקרא רשע וכשהמלוה מכיר את הלוה שהוא בעל מדה זו מוטב שלא להלוותו ממה שילווהו ויצטרך לנגשו אחר כך ויעבור בכל פעם משום לא תהיה לו כנושה:

A borrower is forbidden to take a loan and spend it unnecessarily and squander it to the point where the lender cannot collect his due. If he does this, he is called an evildoer, and if the lender knows that the borrower possesses this tendency [of squandering borrowed money], it is preferable not to lend him money rather than lend him and then have to pressure him later, each time violating the prohibition of, "You shall not act as a creditor to him.

STUDENT RESOURCE 25

MORTGAGE PAYMENTS & INTEREST

(IN-CLASS EXERCISE)

A. Comparative Table

	30-year mortgage 7% interest	30-year mortgage 4.5% interest	15-year mortgage 7% interest	15-year mortgage 4.5% interest	30-year mortgage 4.5% interest
Loan amount	$200,000	$200,000	$200,000	$200,000	$300,000
Annual interest rate	7%	4.5%	7%	4.5%	4.5%
Loan period in years	30	30	15	15	30
Monthly payment	$1,330.60	$1,013.37	$1,797.66	$1,529.99	$1,520.06
Number of payments	360	360	180	180	180
Total interest owed	$279,017.80	$164,813.42	$123,578.18	$75,397.58	$247,220.13
Total money paid (principal + interest)					

B. Questions

1. What are the advantages of a 30-year-loan over a 15-year?
2. What are the advantages of a 15-year-loan over 30-year?
3. In the last row of the above table, fill in the actual amounts repaid over the term of the loan in each of the four scenarios.
4. Chaim and Devora Schwartz have four children, the oldest of whom is an eight-year-old boy. They need a $200,000 mortgage to buy a house, and interest rates are at 4.5%. They can comfortably afford to pay $1200 a month for their mortgage, but paying $1500 a month would be a strain on their budget, and would require them to tighten their belts significantly. What considerations should they take into account when deciding between a 15-year mortgage and a 30-year?
   - **Inflation** – money is worth less over time, so $1500 gets easier to pay over time.
   - **Weddings** – in 15 years, the Schwartzes will likely have children in shidduchim, and they will probably prefer not to have to be paying a mortgage then.
   - **Higher expenses** – as children grow older and the family grows, cost of living increases dramatically.
   - **Higher income** – as people grow older and become more experienced and established in their fields, their income generally increases.
5. Chaim and Devora decide to stretch themselves to pay $1500/month for a 15-year mortgage. Then, they realize that their car is getting old, and their new house can use some renovations. Of course, they also need furniture. Their mortgage broker offers them a $300,000, 30-year mortgage for practically the same monthly payment as the $200,000, 15-year. If you were in their shoes, what would you do? Why?

STUDENT RESOURCE 26

GUIDELINES FOR DEBT MANAGEMENT

Guideline #1: Divide & Conquer

Management of debt has to be separated from management of the family's income and living expenses. Loans cannot be considered income and cannot be used to cover ongoing living expenses. Conversely, money designated for living expenses cannot be used for debt repayment.

Guideline #2: Create a Debt Repayment Timetable

If the family has an annual budget surplus, it should be possible to solve the debt problem. If this amount is insufficient to cover the current monthly debt repayments, it may be necessary to procure interim loans for the family, or to renegotiate or freeze certain debts.

Guideline #3: Consolidate the Debts

The best way to pay off debt is to consolidate all of the debts into one large loan with reasonable repayment terms. The total amount to be repaid each month cannot exceed the amount that the family's annual budget surplus allows it to set aside each month.

Guideline #4: Negotiate with Creditors

If the loans that have been procured do not cover all of the debts, they should contact the creditors and suggest solutions that will ease their burden for the family. Often, creditors will prefer to be flexible with regard to the repayment terms, rather than take a chance of losing their money completely.

STUDENT RESOURCE 26

Guideline #5: Pay the Troublesome or Small Debts First Down to the Last Penny

Generally, interest-bearing debts, or debts that will incur late charges or legal action, should be paid first. Stress can be minimized by getting the smaller debts out of the way first completely.

Guideline #6: Get Help

There are professionals and organizations dedicated to helping people develop strategies for debt repayment. If debt is overwhelming, do not hesitate to get help.

Guideline #7: Seek Rabbinic Guidance

Borrowing money involves many halachic considerations. Before borrowing, and when making repayment arrangements, you should consult with a rav to ensure that your debt management strategies are in consonance with halachah.

Unit 4

Long-Term Financial Planning

Introduction

A household cannot be deemed financially sound if its income and expenses are precisely equal. Financial stability entails planning for the future, as well, such as by putting aside money for unanticipated emergencies, saving up nest-eggs for future simchas and for old-age (though it may seem a million years away!), making safe, long-term investments, and purchasing suitable insurance coverage.

Some people mistakenly equate financial planning with a lack of bitachon. After all, they assert, the Gemara states (*Sotah* 48b), "One who has bread in his basket and says, 'What will I eat tomorrow?' has a minimum of belief."

But Torah sources throughout the ages have declared that setting aside money for the future is a halachic imperative, and is a classic example of the hishtadlus we are required to do, while, at the same time, recognizing that its success hinges totally on Hashem's Will.

In actuality, savings are a loan to yourself. It is no harder to exert yourself to put money away beforehand than it is to repay it afterward. And a "loan" to yourself carries great advantages; it is devoid of interest and spares you the shame of having to be beholden to others.

Goals

- To understand the Torah outlook on savings
- To appreciate the value of having life insurance and understand how it is reconciled with the obligation to have *bitachon*
- To differentiate between wise investments and get-rich-quick schemes and realize that potential gain is always commensurate with degree of risk
- To learn the ins and outs of saving and understand the time value of money
- To become acquainted with the need for a *heter iska* when dealing with business loans/investments
- To apply smart shopping habits to mortgage negotiation
- To learn how to manage existing debts effectively

STUDENT RESOURCE 27

TORAH VIEW ON SAVINGS

מהרש"א חידושי אגדות מסכת נדה דף סה עמוד ב

דיראה אדם להשאיר לו ממון להסתפק ממנו בזקנותו ואל יתן כל נכסיו לבניו בחייו...

The Maharsha states that a person should put aside money for his old age and should not give out all his money to his children in his lifetime.

שו"ת שבט הלוי חלק ד סימן א

...דדבר פשוט דמה שהוא בטבע העולם, כזקנה, ונשואי בניו ובהגיעו לזה אינו לפי כוחותיו להכין כל הנצרך לו אז כזה מצוה להכין בעוד מועד כדי שלא יצטרך לבריות...

In his response Shevet Halevi (4:1), Harav Shmuel Wosner zt"l writes, "It is obvious that [for] something that is the nature of the world, such as old age or marrying off children... it is a mitzvah to prepare in advance, so that he will not become dependent on others."

STUDENT RESOURCE 28

LIFE INSURANCE: TO BUY OR NOT TO BUY?

By Rabbi Yirmiyohu Kaganoff

In Parshas Vayishlach, Yaakov needed to make very important and practical life decisions with major long-term ramifications, when he heard that Esav was approaching with his army of 400 men; these decisions were made based on his halachic and hashkafic background. We also have similar decisions to make. With this introduction, I bring you:

Question 1

Chaim knows that, as the head of the family, he has the responsibility to care for his wife, Fruma, and their children. He feels that this responsibility obligates him to acquire an adequate amount of life insurance should something *chas veshalom* happen to him. Fruma's upbringing was that even discussing this matter can cause bad things to happen. Who is right – Chaim or Fruma?

Question 2

Miriam calls her *rav* with a *shaylah*. "My husband and I would like to buy life insurance, but we're concerned that it might show a lack of bitachon that *Hashem* always does what is best for us. Is that correct?"

* Reprinted with permission from the author.

Question 3

Tzadok is one of the city's biggest *tzaddikim*. He teaches, voluntarily oversees some local *tzedakah* projects, not to mention his incredibly solid *kevi'us itim*. He is a *talmid chacham* and is raising his own large family. One of the *ba'alei batim* has offered to purchase a life insurance policy on his behalf, but Tzadok questions whether doing so might jeopardize him, since his family would no longer be dependent on his support. Is his fear founded?

Answer:

At times we have heard someone opposing life insurance, claiming that it reflects a lack of *bitachon*, or that its acquisition could actually be to one's detriment. Let us understand what the halachic authorities say about this subject. Indeed, are there halachic or hashkafic concerns about purchasing life insurance? From a Torah perspective, should this practice be encouraged or discouraged?

The three situations I presented above demonstrate three different issues that *poskim* discuss when analyzing whether there is a halachic problem in purchasing life insurance. They are:

I. Creating a Devil's Advocate

The *Gemara* states that one should not say something that might cause evil to occur. *Al yiftach adam piv l'satan* – Do not create an opportunity for Satan to mix in! Is purchasing life insurance not considered encouraging the evil Satan to do something nefarious?

II. In G-d We Trust

If we really believe that Hashem provides for all of our needs, doesn't purchasing life insurance demonstrate that we are worried about the future and lack trust in Hashem?

III. Succeeding in Divine Judgment

As opposed to a human court, Hashem's judgment and decisions are perfect, and take all ramifications into consideration. The Heavenly Tribunal will not recall someone unless all the consequences of his disappearance are calculated. Based on this, perhaps purchasing life insurance jeopardizes the insured, since his family is no longer as dependent on his support, thus minimizing the merits he has when judged by the Heavenly Tribunal?

Let's analyze each one of these issues individually, in order to determine whether or not purchasing life insurance should be allowed or even encouraged.

Issue #1: Creating a Devil's Advocate

Al yiftach adam piv l'satan literally translates as, "A person should not open his mouth for Satan." One should be careful not to say something that might provide Satan with ammunition. The *Gemara* applies this rule to forbid a person from saying, "I sinned a lot, but *Hashem* has not punished me." The admission that one is guilty and deserves punishment gives Satan a chance to prosecute one in the Heavenly Tribunal. According to the *Magen Avraham*, the main concern here is that the words "Hashem has not punished me" imply that one anticipates the punishment, although this is clearly not what the speaker intends. However, when Satan prosecutes, he might take the speaker's words out of context.

The question is whether purchasing life insurance provides Satan with such an opportunity to prosecute.

A different Talmudic discussion implies that it is absolutely permissible to make arrangements for oneself in the event of one's demise, and that doing so is not considered opening one's mouth to Satan. The *Gemara* discusses whether someone who prepares for himself shrouds (*tachrichim*) that are four-cornered is required to attach *tzitzis* to their corners, implying that it is, indeed, permitted to prepare shrouds for oneself. In other words, planning for one's death does not constitute violating the warning *al yiftach adam piv l'satan* and does not provide the Satan with any ammunition.

Indeed, this *Gemara's* discussion is rallied as a source in the following situation. Maury Bond is lying on his deathbed on a hot Friday afternoon. There is concern that if he dies before Shabbos, his corpse will begin to decompose and smell unpleasant before it can be buried after Shabbos, which would not be a *kavod* for the departed. (Remember that earlier generations did not have ready access to refrigeration.) The authorities debate whether it is permitted to dig Maury's grave while he is still breathing, so that, should he die on Friday, he could be buried quickly before Shabbos. Most authorities permit digging the grave while Maury is still living; the dissenting opinion prohibits this out of concern that Maury might find out that his grave is already dug, which will distress him, and this itself could lead to his premature demise. However, none of the authorities debating this case is concerned that the efficacy of digging Maury's grave while he is still alive violates *al yiftach adam piv l'satan* and provides Satan with the opportunity to clamor for Maury's swift departure. Some of the authorities who discuss this question explicitly state that it is perfectly acceptable for a healthy person to arrange the digging of his own grave and to prepare his own shrouds, as we see from the above-quoted passage in the *Gemara*. One highly respected authority expressly approves the practice of purchasing adjacent burial plots for a couple, the fact that at least one member is still alive notwithstanding.

Thus, we see that it is not considered *al yiftach adam piv l'satan* when a healthy person makes funeral arrangements for himself, since he is not mentioning his sins and giving Satan any reason to prosecute him. Based on this, several authorities rule that purchasing life insurance is also not a violation of *al yiftach adam piv l'satan*.

However, I would like to note that there are two sources from which it seems that *al yiftach adam piv l'satan* applies in some other cases. In *Kesubos* 8b, the *Gemara* states that a person should not make the following declaration, "Many will drink the cup of mourning" because of the concern of *al yiftach adam piv l'satan*. This source implies that there is concern of *al yiftach adam piv l'satan* even when one's statement does not imply that one has sinned and deserves punishment. Similarly, a different *Gemara* passage states that upon entering the bathhouse (which in those days involved a moderate degree of danger), one should not say, "If something goes wrong, my death should atone for my sins," because of *al yiftach adam piv l'satan*.

Thus, we need to resolve why the halachic authorities who discuss making shrouds, digging a grave, or purchasing a burial plot for a living person do not prohibit these actions because of the principle of *al yiftach adam piv l'satan*, even though the statements, "Many will drink the cup of mourning," and "If something goes wrong, my death should atone for my sins," are prohibited for this reason.

The answer appears to be that these last two cases are a concern only because one is ***expressing*** the possibility of one's passing, which fits the words of *Chazal*: a person should not *say*, "I sinned a lot, but Hashem has not punished me." Assuming our solution is correct, arranging plans for one's demise, including writing one's will and purchasing life insurance would not violate *al yiftach adam piv l'satan*, provided that one does not express verbally the possibility of one's death.

Issue #2:

In G-d We Trust – Exclusively

A Jew is obligated to believe that although he makes an effort to earn his livelihood (*parnassah)*, it is ultimately Hashem alone Who provides it. The question is whether there is a difference between working for one's daily needs and working to save money for future expenses. Is it a shortcoming in *bitachon* to save for the future? Does purchasing life insurance imply lack of confidence that Hashem will provide for his family?

To answer these questions, we must first examine the halachic relationship between *parnassah* and *bitachon*.

Is there a Dispute in the Mishnah?

The Mishnah quotes two ostensibly dissenting opinions. Rabbi Meir is quoted first as saying: "A person should teach his son a livelihood that is easy (to learn) and free of potential sin. (At the same time, he should) pray to Him Who is the source of all wealth and property. (Always realize that) there is no profession that does not have its vicissitudes. Poverty and wealth are dependent on his merit." We see that Rabbi Meir advocates teaching one's child a livelihood, while simultaneously acknowledging that livelihood comes from Hashem and not from our efforts.

On the other hand, the very same mishnah quotes Rabbi Nehorai as saying, "I abandon all means of livelihood and teach my son only Torah."

Thus, we appear to have a dispute between two *tanna'im* as to whether one should take time from teaching one's son Torah in order to provide him with vocational training. However, this analysis cannot be accurate for the following reason:

The *Gemara* teaches that Rabbi Meir was an alternate name for Rabbi Nehorai, because his teaching of Torah produced so much light. (Meir means "He who gives light," and the word Nehorai also means "light".) How could Rabbi Nehorai disagree with himself?

Resolving the Dispute

One answer to this problem is that Rabbi Nehorai's statement that he would teach his son nothing but Torah was personal – Rabbi Nehorai himself had no worldly concerns, because he placed complete trust in Hashem. Someone at this level should indeed not teach his son any worldly occupation. However, most people do not reach this level of trust and must provide their son with a livelihood, while emphasizing that *parnassah* is from Hashem.

Rav Moshe Feinstein presents an alternative answer to the contradictory statements of Rabbi Meir. The two statements are discussing different stages of life, one before the son must begin supporting his family, and the other when he has to support his family. Rabbi Nehorai's statement that "I teach my son only Torah" applies before the son needs *parnassah*. Until then, he should learn only Torah. The other statement refers to a son who has to earn a living. At that point, his father should teach him a livelihood that involves few halachic challenges and is easy to learn, while at the same time teaching him that his vocation is only *hishtadlus*, one's feeble apparent attempt, and that *parnassah* comes only from Hashem.

There is a halachic difference between the two approaches. According to the first approach, someone with total trust that Hashem will provide for him, even if he makes no *hishtadlus*, should not make any effort toward *parnassah*. According to Rav Moshe's approach, even a person with total trust in Hashem is required to have a livelihood. Rav Moshe brings evidence from several sources that it is inappropriate to rely on miracles for one's *parnassah*. Furthermore, he considers having no livelihood as equivalent to relying on miracles.

On the other hand, Rav Vozner rules, similarly to the first approach, that a pure *baal-bitachon* is permitted to rely totally on Hashem for *parnassah*; however, he agrees that this applies only to rare individuals. There are stories about *Gedolim*, such as Rav Yosef Chayim Sonnenfeld, who made no conventional *hishtadlus* to attain *parnassah*. These *Gedolim*, too, must have had the same opinion as Rav Vozner. According to Rav Moshe's approach, one may not deliberately adopt such a lifestyle.

Both Rav Moshe and Rav Vozner rule that, generally speaking, people are required to have some type of *parnassah*, and that it is not a lack of *bitachon* to do so. Unless he is a great *tzaddik*, no one should assume that he has sufficient *zechuyos* (merits) to expect Hashem to provide his *parnassah* with no *hishtadlus* whatsoever on his part.

The *poskim* bring evidence from *Tosafos* that it is not a shortcoming to make arrangements to take care of one's financial future. The *Gemara* rules that although a father has the halachic ability to marry off his daughter while she is a minor, he is prohibited to do so out of concern that when she grows up, she may not like her husband. In *Tosafos*' time, however, underage daughters were married off, which appeared to be a violation of this halacha. Upon what basis was there a practice contrary to the *Gemara's* ruling?

Tosafos explains that in his turbulent times (the *Baalei Tosafos* lived during the period of the Crusades), a man who had sufficient means to provide his daughter with a dowry, should arrange her marriage to someone appropriate. If the father delayed, he risked losing his money, which could have been tantamount to his becoming unable to marry off his daughter. *Tosafos* does not contend that a person should have *bitachon* that he will have the means to be able to marry her off later.

Similarly, someone who can purchase life insurance, an annuity, or other means for making his life or the lives of his dependents more secure, may do so. *Bitachon* does not require someone to ignore future needs. *Bitachon* does require that a person realize that everything that happens is under Hashem's supervision and control.

What Will I Eat Tomorrow?

But doesn't this approach violate the statement that "Someone who has (today's) bread in his basket, and asks, 'What will I eat tomorrow?' lacks faith"? Aren't *Chazal* teaching us that someone who plans for tomorrow's livelihood lacks proper trust in Hashem?

The answer is no. This last passage is

discussing people's beliefs. Everyone must believe that Hashem provides for him and that whatever happens is under His control. One may not say, "What will I eat tomorrow?" thereby ignoring Hashem's supervision. However, this does not mean that making practical plans for the future is a violation of *bitachon*, provided one fully realizes that everything comes from Hashem and is dependent on Him.

The Manna

However, there is another passage of *Gemara* that may indicate otherwise:

"Rabbi Shimon ben Yochai's disciples asked him, 'Why did the manna not fall for the *B'nei Yisrael* once a year (for the entire year)?' He answered them, 'I will give you a parable. A human king once provided his son with support on an annual basis. The son visited his father once a year to receive his allowance. Wanting to see his son more often, the father altered the system and began providing his son with support on a daily basis. Thereafter, his son visited his father every day. Similarly, the head of a large household worried that no manna would fall on the morrow; thus he would pray daily for sustenance." Doesn't this *Gemara* imply that it is better for one's *parnassah* to arrive one day at a time than to plan for the future?

The halachic authorities provide two answers to this question that are dependent on the dispute between Rav Vozner and Rav Moshe mentioned earlier. According to Rav Vozner, this *Gemara* reflects the ideal: a great *tzaddik* should indeed receive his *parnassah* one day at a time. However, most people are not at this level of faith and may plan for the future. According to Rav Moshe's approach, the *Gemara* means that a person should mentally acknowledge every day that Hashem provides for all his needs; however, he is permitted and required to make *hishtadlus*, which includes planning for future needs. It should be noted that all the *poskim* that I have seen discussing this issue rule that purchasing life insurance qualifies as normal *hishtadlus*.

In this context, it is worthwhile to quote a *Midrash* that demonstrates the obligation to make *hishtadlus*. Quoting the *pasuk*, "*L'ma'an yevorechecha Hashem Elokecha b'chol ma'asecha asher ta'aseh*," "So that Hashem Your G-d will bless you in all your deeds that you will perform," the *Midrash* points out that the last two words of the *posuk*, *"asher taaseh,"* "that you will perform" are seemingly superfluous, because the Torah already stated, *"b'chol ma'asecha,"* "in all your deeds." What is added with the words, "that you will perform?"

The *Midrash* explains, "The Torah states, 'Keep the mitzvos.' I might think that he should do nothing and expect his *parnassah* to come automatically? Therefore, the Torah repeats, 'that you will perform.' If you work, you will receive blessing, and if you do not work, you will not receive blessing." This *Midrash* proves that one has a responsibility to earn *parnassah*.

Issue #3: Succeeding in Divine Judgment

I have heard people give yet another reason why someone should not purchase life insurance. What happens if a husband does not have the personal merit to guarantee longevity, while his wife and children do have the merit or the *mazel* (fortune) to live financially secure lives? In a case like this, the husband would live a long productive life as their provider. By purchasing life insurance, which guarantees their sustenance even without his presence, he jeopardizes his life, since his dependents are now provided for should something bad happen to him.

In the one halachic source that I saw mention this concern, the author, Rav Yitzchok Sternhell *zt"l*, quoted the exact opposite approach in the name of the Shinaver Rav (Rav Yechezkel Shraga Halberstam *zt"l*, author of *Divrei Yechezkel*), who was one of the greatest halachic authorities of his day in Galicia. The Shinaver contended that buying life insurance should provide longevity. He argues that since the *mazel* of the people who own insurance companies is to become wealthy, their *mazel* will prevail and prevent them from losing money by having to pay out life insurance policies. Thus, purchasing a policy actually rallies *mazel* to one's side and does not jeopardize one's life.

Another counter-argument runs as follows: If loss of merit is a concern, then there is valid reason to refrain from accumulating any wealth. The family members of a man who ekes out a daily existence are far more dependent on their breadwinner than are the wife and children of a wealthy man, since he will leave them with an appreciable inheritance should something happen to him. Thus, one could argue that accumulating wealth is not in one's best interest, an approach that does not have too many advocates. I have never seen anyone refrain from accumulating wealth because of this concern, and neither have I seen any halachic authority suggest this as a reason to avoid affluence. Therefore, I conclude that this is not a factor in the question of purchasing life insurance.

In conclusion, I am aware of thirteen written *teshuvos* (responsa) on the purchase of life insurance or annuities, written by authorities representing *Litvishe, Chassidishe* and Sefardic approaches. All thirteen *teshuvos* permit purchasing life insurance, and some encourage the practice strongly.

Rav Meir Shapiro, the rosh yeshiva of Yeshivas Chachmei Lublin, had a very large life insurance policy, even though he unfortunately had no children. His reason was that since fundraising for the yeshiva was completely on his shoulders, he was concerned that in the event of his premature death, the yeshiva would be forced to close. We see that he was not concerned with any of the above issues and felt that purchasing insurance was an appropriate course of action. ***May we all be blessed with long years and good health.***

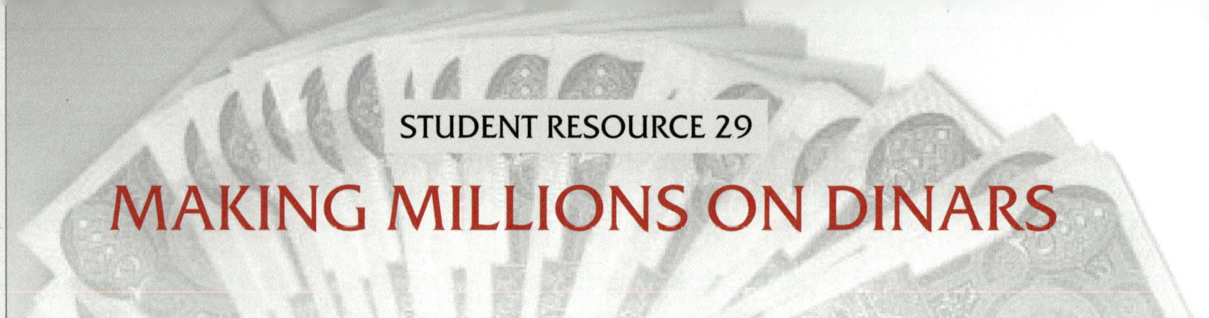

STUDENT RESOURCE 29

MAKING MILLIONS ON DINARS

Q: *A yungerman in the kollel where I learn recently showed me an article describing the exciting new possibility of investing in Iraqi dinars. The article said that until 1982, the Iraqi dinar was worth about $3, and today, one million Iraqi dinars can be bought for only $700. The value of the dinar is sure to rise when the conflict in Iraq is resolved, and my friends tell me that I can invest a few thousand dollars in Iraqi dinars and come out with millions of dollars when the dinar goes up. I have some money put aside that I was looking to invest. I know many yungeleit who have invested in these dinars, and I am wondering if I should do the same. Do you think this is a worthwhile investment?*

A: We at Mesila are not licensed investment advisors, and we are therefore not qualified to guide you with regard to the specifics of investments. For investment advice, we suggest that you contact a licensed financial professional such as Hamodia investment columnist Aaron Katsman, who happens to be an active Mesila volunteer counselor.

We also do not wish to discuss the issue of whether it is appropriate for a *ben Torah* to busy himself with investment opportunities, although we would certainly hope that your *kollel* studies focus on disputes between Abaye and Rava, not on the finer points of the conflict between the Shiites and the Sunnis.

Mesila's mission, and the objective of this column, is to convey responsible, Torah-based attitudes towards finances. We will therefore attempt to expose the fallacies inherent in get-rich-quick schemes, the Iraqi dinar craze in particular.

From the time Adam Harishon was cursed, "By the sweat of your brow shall you eat bread," earning a livelihood has been a struggle for mankind. There are no exemptions from this curse, and promises of easy money are always – *always* – misleading.

For someone learning in *kollel*, investing might seem like the ideal way to earn *parnassah* effortlessly, without ever having to leave the *beis medrash*. All you have to do is put your money into a surefire investment, and you are set. Well, it does not quite work that way.

Investing, by definition, means risking capital for the sake of an anticipated future gain, or return. As a rule, return is directly proportional to risk – the greater the risk, the higher the potential return. The converse is true as well: the higher the potential return, the greater the risk. If someone promises you returns of millions of dollars on an investment of thousands, you can be sure of two things: (1) the risk is far too high to justify the investment, and (2) the person is either very naïve or a con artist.

Get-rich-quick schemes lure people with the promise of high returns and no risk. But wise investors know that any investment that cannot go down, cannot go up either. Never believe anyone who tells you that an investment is sure to go up. If it is sure to go up, there would be no risk – and without risk, there can be no significant returns.

Currency speculation is a particularly risky form of investment, because it is difficult to predict the movements of any currency, even established ones. Given the volatility of the Iraqi economy, we would not place much confidence in the prospects of its fledgling currency.

What makes you and your *kollel* buddies sure that the dinar will go up? How do you know that it will not be devalued to even less than its current value? And why are you so confident that the conflict in Iraq will be successfully resolved?

Even if Iraqi dinars were worth investing in at some point, you can be sure that by the time you heard about the prospect in your *kollel*, the market price for dinars would have already corrected itself to reflect the latest speculative excitement and the resulting demand.

"Buy the rumor, sell the news" is an old principle of investing. Basically, it means that you should only put your money into an investment before it makes the headlines, not when everyone else has already heard about it and bought in. The new Iraqi dinar has been around since 2003, and has long ceased to be the hot rumor; it is not even news anymore.

Furthermore, there is no real market for Iraqi dinars nowadays. It is therefore unlikely that you will be able to sell your dinars at a profit; you might not even be able to liquidate them at all. And because dinars are not a very commonly traded currency, you will have to pay high commissions and change fees when purchasing them. So you are basically guaranteed a loss the moment you get your hands on any dinars.

Putting your money into Iraqi dinars, or any other "can't lose" proposition, is not investing, but gambling. As such, it cannot even be considered part of your requisite *hishtadlus* for *parnassah*. You would do your friends a service by cautioning them against buying Iraqi dinars and explaining to them that there is no such thing as easy money.

Common sense would dictate that you keep your money far away from anything remotely related to Iraq, and spare yourself the pain of watching your money disappear. As for your friends who have already invested in Iraqi dinars, we hope that they lose enough money early on to discourage them from dabbling blindly in speculative investments ever again.

Having dealt with many clients who lost everything in the process of getting rich quick, Mesila strongly discourages people from investing their money without the help of an investment professional. An investment professional will assess your complete financial situation, determine the level of risk appropriate for you, and help you find the investments that are right for you.

Reprinted from *Your Money and Your Life: Mesila's Down-to-Earth, Torah-Based Strategies for Managing Your Finances*, by M. Heimowitz

STUDENT RESOURCE 30

THE MYTH OF GUARANTEED RETURNS

Question: *When I got married about a year ago, my parents and in-laws put together a nice sum of money for us to live on for several years, and suggested that I invest it. I found out about a very promising real estate project that offered 18% interest and had very wealthy, reliable guarantors offering their personal guarantee. I invested the money into that project, and for the first few months after I invested, I was able to pay my rent with the interest. Then a problem arose with the project, and for the past three months, I have not received any interest payments. I have requested that my capital be returned, but a few weeks have passed and I have not received any money back.*

I recently heard about another real estate project that pays only 16% interest, but will give me a lien on the property as a guarantee. When I get my capital back, I hope to invest in this project, but in the meantime, I need money to pay my rent. Would it be advisable for me to borrow money to invest in this second project, in view of the fact that I have a solid guarantee to borrow against? One other question – at what point would it be appropriate for me to approach the guarantors of the first project?

A: Your situation is reminiscent of Chazal's saying, *Mi she'achal shum, yachzor v'yochal shum?* – if someone ate garlic (and is suffering from bad breath), should he go and eat more garlic (*Shabbos* 31b)?

You were burned once with a real estate investment that sounded, and was, too good to be true. Even if you had more of your own money to invest, why would you take a chance of getting burned again?

As a rule, you should be wary of any investment that offers returns higher than those paid by the bank. (Government bonds are the notable exception; they pay more than the bank, but are generally considered a safe investment.)

Phrases like "guaranteed returns" and "no risk" so often dupe novice investors into naively believing that they can invest their money, and voila, their financial worries will be over. At Mesila, we see the devastating results of this naïveté time and time again.

Although we do not know the details of either of the projects you describe, we can safely assume that any investments that promise such high returns are too risky. This assumption is based on the premise that anyone looking for investment capital would prefer to borrow at bank lending rates than at 16-18%. If a real estate project is offering returns of 16% on your money, you can be sure that no bank was willing to sink money into the project. Is your tolerance for risk, or risk appetite, greater than the bank's? Considering the fact that you do not have money to pay your rent, we think not.

In our opinion, it would be unconscionable for anyone to borrow money to invest in an enterprise as risky as the projects you have described. The lien you have been offered on the second property does not guarantee anything; if the property would be enough of a loan guarantee, the bank would have been very willing to take it as collateral, and there would have been no need for private investors like yourself. Do not let the offer of the lien blind you into risking more capital, especially if the money is borrowed. If you lose the capital – and with such high risk, there is a good chance that you *will* lose the capital – how will you repay the loan?

The money you invested in the first project is not money you can count on, and definitely not money you can borrow against. While we certainly hope that you will get back your money, you should be prepared for the possibility that it may take years of wrangling and legal action before you see a penny of it.

In answer to your second question, we recommend that you approach the guarantors of the first project immediately, before they are inundated with demands from other creditors. The fact that these guarantors were once wealthy and reliable is no assurance that they will be able to bear the financial backlash of a failed real estate proposition. You should therefore make sure that you are one of the first in line to receive any money that might be forthcoming.

As a final note, we wish to stress that risking capital for the promise of high returns is not only unwise from an investment standpoint, but is problematic from a Torah perspective as well. Yaakov Avinu went back across the Yabok River to retrieve some small jugs, the Midrash tells us, because *tzaddikim* value their money. The *sefer Beer Yosef* explains that the reason *tzaddikim* value their money is not because they ascribe importance to material acquisition; rather, it is because they understand that everything they own is a gift from Hashem, and if Hashem gives a person something, he has an obligation to take care of it and use it properly.

When people put money into risky investments, it shows a certain disregard for the *hashgacha pratis* that decreed that the money should be theirs.

In your case, the capital you invested, and now wish to re-invest, is the hard-earned money given to you by your loving parents and in-laws. *Hakaras hatov* would dictate that you should be exceedingly careful not to squander this money.

When you do get back your capital, we urge you to seek the advice of a licensed financial advisor before you invest it again.

STUDENT RESOURCE 31

SAVINGS: THE LONG AND SHORT OF IT

Question: *I earn a respectable income, and I am B"H able to support my family adequately. We live relatively simply, and I don't think that we waste money on unnecessary purchases. The problem is that we can't seem to put anything aside for the future. Besides for our mortgage, we are not in debt, but we have no savings to speak of and we never have any extra money to put away for savings. This worries me tremendously. I know that financial experts say that people should save up for retirement and other future needs, and I would love to follow this advice, but frankly, saving money just seems like an impossible goal. Do you have any ideas for me?*

A: The first step towards successfully saving for the future is having an appreciation for the value and importance of savings. Your concern over your present inability to save is a clear indication that you do possess this appreciation, and we therefore think that a bit of guidance is all you need in order to begin saving.

Saving for the future makes sense financially, but it is not only financial experts who advocate saving for the future. The Maharsha states in his *Chiddushei Aggados* (*Niddah* 65b) that a person should put aside money for his old age. In his Responsa *Shevet Halevi* (4:1), Harav Shmuel Wosner *shlita* writes, "It is obvious that [for] something that is the nature of the world, such as old age or marrying off children… it is a mitzvah to prepare in advance so that he will not become dependent on others."

Clearly, then, it is incumbent upon every Jewish family to plan for their financial future and save up money to cover future needs.

How to Start Saving

Like you, many people tell Mesila that they are barely managing financially – or not managing at all – and that they cannot even begin to think about saving. But saving is not something you do when you have extra money. There *is* no such thing as "extra" money – no matter how much money a person has, there are always demands made on that money.

Saving is simply a habit. It is a habit that for some people comes naturally, and for others has to be learned. How do you get into the habit of savings? Here are some pointers for getting started:

› **Start small**. Put aside your pocket change at the end of the day, put aside $10 a week, or put aside 5% of your monthly paycheck – just save something. *Prutah prutah mitztarefes* – if you save consistently, the amounts will eventually add up. More important, saving small amounts regularly will get you into the habit of saving in a way that is almost painless.

› **Save now**. You will always have good reasons not to save. Don't let these good reasons stop you from putting away at least something. (A caveat to this pointer – if you are carrying high-interest debt – credit card debt, for instance – your priority should be debt repayment, and not savings. A balance on your credit card might cost you 18% interest – and that's a lot more than you'll earn on most savings plans or investments.)

- **Save your windfalls.** Any time unexpected money comes your way – in the form of product rebates, tax refunds, gifts, etc. – put at least a portion of it towards savings immediately.
- **Make savings automatic.** You can set up a savings plan that will withdraw a certain amount of money from your bank account every month, or you can arrange for a portion of your paycheck to go directly to savings. This way, you barely feel the pinch.
- **Save first.** The first expense that comes off your paycheck should be your savings. Too many people say that they will save what is left at the end of the month. Those are the people who never manage to save anything.
- **Make it a team effort.** Both husband and wife – and possibly children as well, depending on their ages – need to be actively involved in the savings habit in order for it to work.
- **Watch where the money goes.** People who keep track of where their money goes end up spending less and saving more. Knowing how you are spending your money gives you more control over your expenditures and helps you to make better spending decisions. This leaves you with more money to save. It also gives you the freedom to decide how to use your money, rather than allowing spending pressures to dictate where your money goes.

Once you have decided to start saving, the next step is to decide what to do with your savings. There are two important categories of savings: short-term and long-term. Each of these requires a different strategy.

Short-Term Savings

This is the money you'll need for emergencies and for foreseeable large expenses.

Everyone needs some short-term savings. If you don't have any short-term savings, even minor financial setbacks can have disastrous results. A burst pipe, or even something as predictable as summer camp, can land you in debt or force you to sell or forfeit some of your assets. You would not want to lose your house or your car because you are temporarily unable to make the payments.

Short-term savings can earn enough interest to keep up with inflation, but will never yield the high returns associated with higher-risk investments. When choosing a home for your short-term savings, your primary considerations should be accessibility, liquidity and safety of principal.

Where should you keep your short-term savings? In a place that is accessible enough to dip into in a time of real need yet not accessible enough to spend any time you run out of cash. We recommend that you put short-term savings in a separate bank account, in a trustworthy *gemach*, or in very low-risk investments such as money market accounts, money market funds, certificates of deposit, high-interest savings accounts (available at certain banks and financial institutions) or treasury bonds. Each of these options has its pros and cons, but all of them are relatively safe, relatively liquid (easy to convert to cash), and earn relatively low interest.

Your should *not* put your short-term savings in higher-risk investments such as stocks, commodities or real estate.

How much money should you keep in short-term savings? That depends on your situation and your family's needs. Financial professionals usually recommend setting aside at least three months' worth of living expenses to tide you over in the event of an emergency or temporary unemployment or disability.

Besides for this emergency fund, you should also save for expenses looming on the horizon: your annual car insurance bill, the sputtering refrigerator that will need to be replaced soon, your son's bar mitzvah, and so on. These expenses are all predictable, and you have two choices how to pay for them: save up money and *earn* interest, or borrow the money and *pay* interest (at a much higher rate).

Long-Term Savings

Long-term savings is the money you'll need for times of considerable financial strain, such as marrying off children and old age.

When choosing a home for your long-term savings, remember that inflation reduces the value of your money by about 3% a year. By keeping your long-term savings under your mattress, you actually lose money. It is therefore important to put your money in a place where it will earn respectable returns. That is why the term "investing" is used much more with regard to long-term savings than with regard to short-term savings.

With long-term savings, you have the opportunity to let your investments earn compound interest (interest on interest), which effortlessly multiplies your investment. But compound interest needs time to work its magic.

To illustrate: If you save $2,000 a year for 40 years (a total savings of $80,000) and earn interest of 8% annually, you will have $559,562 by the time you are finished. If you save $2,000 a year for 30 years (a total savings of $60,000) at the same interest rate of 8%, you will end up with $244,692 – less than half. (For comparison's sake, saving the same amount at an interest rate of 5% would give you $253,680 after 40 years and $139,522 after 30 years.)

Here's another example. Let's say you want to save about $50,000 for your son's wedding. If your son is a newborn, you need to save $100 a month at 8% for 18 years (a total savings of $21,600) to have that amount. If your son is 13, you will need to save $430 a month for 7 years at 8% (a total savings of $36,120) to have that same $50,000 by the time he turns 20.

People in their 20s don't usually think much about marrying off their children or about their retirement, but if they would, they would reap the rewards later. When you are young, you can invest relatively little and wind up with far more money than someone older who saves much more.

The simplest way to start saving for retirement is to sign up for your employer's pension plan (known as a 401(k) in the U.S.). If this is not an option, you should speak to a financial adviser about starting your own tax-deferred savings plan (known as an IRA in the U.S.). People in Israel should speak to an insurance agent who specializes in pension planning.

Putting money into stocks and stock funds – a terrible idea for short-term savings – is actually a very good idea for long-term savings. The stock market is notorious for its volatility, but over the past 80 years it has yielded an average return of about 10% – higher than any other type of investment.

Another advantage of the stock market is that you have the option of investing even minimal amounts. Even if you cannot afford to put away a lot of money, you can still enjoy the long-term benefits of stock market investments.

Higher returns like those associated with the stock market usually involve higher risks. When you are investing for the long term, however, you are able to accept more risk. Since time is on your side, you have the ability to ride out the ups and downs of the economy without being affected every time the market takes a hit.

When investing in the stock market, we strongly discourage active investing or day trading. The approach we advocate is "buy and hold," in which you allow your portfolio to grow over time without selling or exchanging specific investments.

To minimize your risks, it is important to maintain a diversified investment portfolio. This is in keeping with Chazal's advice (*Bava Metzia* 42b) to keep a third of your assets in real estate, a third in merchandise, and a third liquid.

Diversification ensures that your financial future is not dependent on the performance of any one investment. Mutual funds (including index funds and retirement funds) are a common type of diversified investment, although not all mutual funds are created equal.

A good investment portfolio contains a mixture of stocks, bonds and real estate investments. The exact mixture should be determined based on your level of risk tolerance, which depends on factors such as your present financial situation, your future financial goals, and the age and number of your dependents. We recommend that you work with a licensed financial advisor to decide what types of investments are appropriate for you.

As you approach the time when you are going to need to withdraw money from long-term savings, financial experts recommend that you shift some of your holdings into bonds, which are considered less profitable but also less volatile than stocks. In this way, you are protected if the stock market suddenly crashes just before you need to dip into your savings.

In comparison to stocks and bonds, certain real estate and business investments require a much larger initial outlay and a far more sophisticated investment strategy. Novice investors should steer clear of these types of investments, which necessitate professional evaluation, extensive research, a thorough understanding of the market, and a high level of risk tolerance.

Once you have started a long-term savings plan, stick with it. There will always be new investment possibilities on the horizon that sound more exciting and promise higher returns, but in the end, the simple, steady and boring usually outperforms the new, exciting and lucrative.

It's never too late – or too early – to start saving for the future. The key is to determine what your savings goals are, and to start – today!

Reprinted from *Your Money and Your Life: Mesila's Down-to-Earth, Torah-Based Strategies for Managing Your Finances*, by M. Heimowitz

THE MAGIC OF COMPOUND INTEREST
OR
THE TIME VALUE OF MONEY

Once upon a time, Gila and Rina were 17-year-old twin sisters in high school who did a lot of babysitting in their spare time. Their grandmother promised to match any money they saved up in an IRA (IRA: A personal retirement plan that enjoys special tax benefits), which was paying 7.5% compound interest (don't forget, this is a fairy tale).

Gila managed to put aside $600 a year, which her grandmother matched, for a total of $1200, and they continued this arrangement for 10 years.

Rina, in the meantime, drank a lot of iced coffee. When she decided to cut down on caffeine 10 years later, at age 27, she found herself with some extra cash, and she too began to take advantage of Bubby's largesse. She opened her own IRA and put away $1200 for the next 24 years, until Bubby passed away.

At that point, Gila and Rina decided to take a peek at their accounts and see how much money was in there.

Table A

At age	Gila saves	Rina saves
17	$1200	$0
18	$1200	$0
19	$1200	$0
20	$1200	$0
21	$1200	$0
22	$1200	$0
23	$1200	$0
24	$1200	$0
25	$1200	$0
26	$1200	$0

Table B

At age	If Gila stops saving	If Gila continues saving	Rina starts saving
27	$0	$1200	$1200
28	$0	$1200	$1200
29	$0	$1200	$1200
30	$0	$1200	$1200
31	$0	$1200	$1200
32	$0	$1200	$1200
33	$0	$1200	$1200
34	$0	$1200	$1200
35	$0	$1200	$1200
36	$0	$1200	$1200
37	$0	$1200	$1200
38	$0	$1200	$1200
39	$0	$1200	$1200
40	$0	$1200	$1200
41	$0	$1200	$1200
42	$0	$1200	$1200
43	$0	$1200	$1200
44	$0	$1200	$1200
45	$0	$1200	$1200
46	$0	$1200	$1200
47	$0	$1200	$1200
48	$0	$1200	$1200
49	$0	$1200	$1200
50	$0	$1200	$1200
Total IRA contribution:	$12,000	$40,000	$28,000
Total account value:	**$96,307**	**$169,872**	**$73,566**

Look at what happened:

Gila's contribution in the first 10 years, totaling $12,000, grows to $96,307 by age 50 – even if she stops contributing at age 26. Rina, who begins investing at age 27, contributes a total of $28,000 over 24 years, but her account value at age 50 is still less than Gila's. Rina contributed more than twice as much money but still hasn't caught up with Gila – all because she procrastinated. The story of Gila and Rina illustrates the magic of compounding interest, or the time value of money.

Our example uses an IRA as a savings plan, but the principle is true regardless of what type of investment account you have. The moral of the story: Start saving *now*.

STUDENT RESOURCE 33

HETER ISKA FORM FOR LOANS
sample

The undersigned ______________________________ ("the Manager")

acknowledges receipt of $ ______________________ ("the Funds")

from ____________________________________ ("the Investor")

The Manager obligates himself to invest the amount of the Funds on behalf of the Investor in a ny investment or to assign to the Investor a proportionate share of the Manager's assets. If the Manager pays the Investor a return equal to % per annum on the Funds together with an amount equal to the Investor's usual fees, benefits, and charges for providing funds if applicable (collectively called "the Yield"), and repays the Funds in accordance with and at the times stipulated in the attached Schedule and pays the full amount of the Funds and any accrued and unpaid Yield, to be fully paid to the Investor by the Maturity date __________, then the Manager shall not be obligated to provide to the Investor any accounting of profits or losses and the Manager shall be entitled to retain all profits in excess of the Yield as the Manager's compensation. The Manager will notify the Investor, in writing, of the amount of the profits or losses on Friday of each week, and in the absence of such notice, the Yield will be deemed to have been earned. If the Yield is not earned in any week, the Investor may call for immediate repayment of the Funds and any accrued and unpaid Yield. The Manager agrees that any claim for loss of any part of the Funds may only be proved by the testimony of two witnesses admissible in accordance with the strictest Orthodox Jewish law before a duly constituted Orthodox Rabbinical Court comprising such rabbis as the Investor may designate in good faith. The Manager agrees that any claim of failure to achieve the Yield shall be binding on the Investor only if the absolute precise amount is proved by an oath of the Manager pursuant to the provision of the strictest Orthodox Jewish law. Such oath shall be of the most onerous of the many forms of oath provided by Orthodox Jewish law, to be taken by the Manager during the course of the reading of the Torah, in such Orthodox Synagogue as may be designated by the Investor, and in the attendance of the Rabbi, the full congregation then in attendance, and a valid Orthodox Rabbinical Court. Failing proof of aforesaid as to the loss of Funds or failure to achieve the Yield, the Funds and the Yield shall be deemed owing as and when due, as set out herein, and the Manager shall be obligated to pay such amounts. Any unpaid portion of the Funds or the Yield shall be deemed reinvested in accordance with the terms of this *heter iska*, both before and after the Maturity Date. This document shall supersede the provisions of any other agreement between the parties which may be inconsistent with this *heter iska*. However, if a Mortgage or other security ("the Security") has been provided by the Manager to the Investor, it shall serve to secure the Manager's obligations hereunder, and the rights and remedies set out in and arising under the Security may be enforced by the Investor in such manner as provided for it in the event of a default by the Manager, subject only to the Manager's right to prove loss of Funds or failure to achieve the Yield, in the manner set out above.

Dated and signed this __________ day of ________ , _______ (year),

in the city of _______________ .

Investor ________________________ Manager ________________________

Assignments

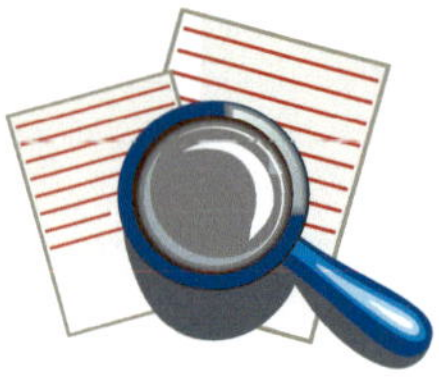

Assignment #1:
Priorities and Spending Attitudes

Objective:

To examine the differing needs and wants among people from different generations, societies, or backgrounds.

Instructions:

1. Choose two interviewees who come from different backgrounds. (Note: The more different your interviewees, the easier this assignment will be for you.)
2. Develop interview questions (8-10) pertaining to spending attitudes and habits, as well as their decision-making process in their purchases. You may use some or all of the sample questions below, but you must also develop some of your own.
    a. What do you consider a need that others might consider a want? What luxuries can you live without that others might consider a necessity?
    b. How did the society you grew up in shape your personal needs and wants?
    c. What did you lack growing up that you wish until this day that you had had? What did you lack growing up that you feel made you into a better person?
    d. Was there ever a time that you lacked something that you absolutely needed? How did you manage?
    e. What's the biggest mistake you think people make when it comes to spending money?
    f. Can you think of a time that you decided not to buy something even though you had the money for it and it was something you could have used?
    g. What do you think is the best advice a parent can give their child about spending?

3. Write an essay (2-3 pages) on one of the following topics.

a. **Topic #1:** Compare and contrast the answers of your two interviewees. How did their differing backgrounds impact their spending and decision-making habits?

b. **Topic #2:** "Our luxuries become our children's necessities." Explain this statement, and state whether you agree or disagree with it, using examples from your two interviewees.

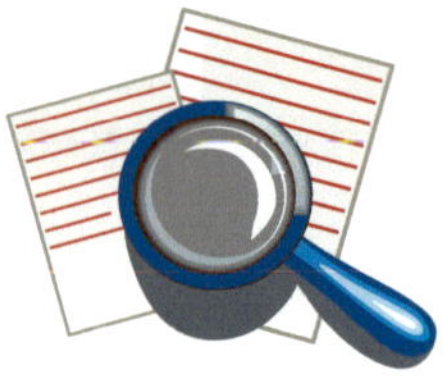

Assignment #2:
You be the Financial Advisor

Mesila's Common Sense Rules for Investors

1. If something sounds too good to be true, it probably is.
2. People who try to get rich quick often lose a lot of money quick.
3. If someone is pressuring you to invest and telling you that the opportunity can't wait, you'd better wait.
4. High returns = high risk. The more money you stand to make, the more money you stand to lose. (If the risks would be low, they wouldn't have to offer such high returns in order to entice people to invest with them.)
5. Bank investments (savings accounts, CDs, etc.) are considered risk-free. Any investment that pays higher returns than the bank is not risk free. But without any risk, you cannot earn more than the bank offers.
6. For every person, there is an appropriate level of risk, depending on how much they can afford to lose. You can take risks only if you are prepared and able to deal with the worst-case scenario (which might mean losing your entire investment, part of it, or having your money tied up for an extended period).
7. "Buy the rumor, sell the news": A hot stock tip that's already public knowledge or is being advertised in the paper is not likely to bring any meaningful returns.
8. Sometimes, a seemingly good investment may be overpriced, which means that you are unlikely to realize any significant returns. A good investment is one that is worth the money you are investing; a bad investment is one for which you overpay.
9. Investments that are based on loopholes or wheeler-dealer schemes are usually not stable investments. Stable investments generally provide some product or service that advances people's needs in some way.
10. Good businessmen and seasoned investors do not need yeshiva students (or the like) to recruit capital for them, and solid investment opportunities are usually snapped up long before they reach the doors of a yeshiva. The types of business

deals and investment opportunities that make it through the doors of yeshivos are often the types that are suited to gullible people only.

11. You have more to lose when investing with a friend or relative than with a stranger. With a stranger, all you can lose is money – with a friend, you can lose a friendship as well.

12. Before investing, do your due diligence. That means carefully investigating the opportunity and consulting with professionals and financial advisors regarding the particular opportunity so that you fully understand the risks involved and are equipped to make informed decisions.

This is a situation that a fellow named Sruli presented to Mesila (details have been changed):

Moish, an old friend of mine, recently approached me at the yeshiva where I learn with a very exciting investment opportunity. Moish's father owns an apartment building that is currently being rented to low-income tenants. He wants to renovate the apartments so that he can rent them out to higher-income tenants for double the rent. "Whatever money you invest with my father will triple in under five years," Moish promises. "But you need to hurry! The bank approved financing for this project, but my father needs investors to sign up within 48 hours – otherwise, the financing will fall through."

When I asked Moish whether the plan had any possible risks, he looked hurt. "This is a foolproof plan," he assured me. "Anyone with a little business sense would understand that in a minute. We just need to make sure that we can get rid of all the old tenants and get the building back up to 95% occupancy within six months. But that should be a cinch."

I know Moish well, and he is a reliable person and a capable businessman. Would you recommend that I invest with him?

Part 1.

Analyze the pros and cons of this investment opportunity. Think ahead. What difficulties may Moish and his father encounter with their plan? Does the plan involve any legal or ethical issues or potential pitfalls?

Part 2.

Referring to Mesila's Ten Common Sense Rules for Investors, which rules would Sruli be following were he to invest with Moish? Which rules would he be breaking?

Part 3.

Using your answers to parts 1 & 2, write a response to Sruli's query advising him whether to invest with Moish. (1-2 pages)

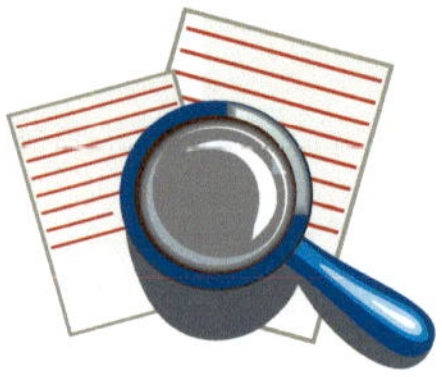

Assignment #3:

Making Informed Credit Card Choices

Assignment: You be the Financial Advisor

Getting a credit card offer in the mail can be exciting. Credit card companies think so, apparently – why else would they send out eight billion offers a year? (That's more than the number of people on the planet.)

But not all offers are created equal. Many people have fallen into the credit card trap and found themselves paying fees they never knew existed. That's why Senator Charles Schumer introduced into law a page of clearly stated disclosures and policies for every credit card. This "Schumer's Box" is now included in every credit card in the U.S.

Before signing up for your preapproved card, with fantastic miles programs and other perks, let's take a look at some different offers and see what makes some cards better than others.

Assignment:

1. Compare the disclosure box ("Schumer's box") of three different credit card offers.
2. What is your introductory interest rate on purchases (APR) and when does the introductory period expire?
3. What happens to your interest rate (APR) if you make one late payment?
4. Does the card have an annual fee? How much?
5. What is the interest rate on cash advances?
6. When does the company begin to charge interest on purchases? When does the company begin to charge interest on cash advances? If there is a difference, explain why it may be significant to the consumer.
7. Is there any circumstance under which the credit card company might change the interest rate?
8. What other factors make one card more attractive than the others?
9. Overall, which card do you recommend, and why?
10. In the absence of the Schumer's box, what information might the consumer have missed?

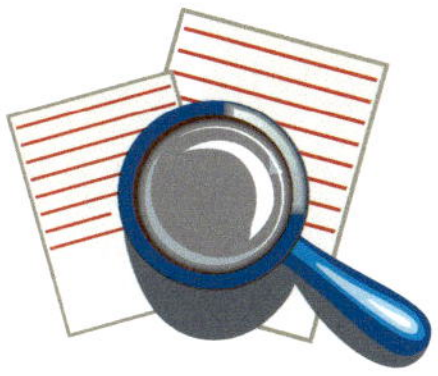

Assignment #4:
Home Ownership Considerations

Scenario

Motti and Dini Hirsch are married eight years, with three children. They are currently renting a 3-bedroom apartment for $1200/month, and they would like to buy a house. The house that they're looking at is in passable condition, priced at $335,000, and is situated on the outskirts of a growing frum community.

Considerations

Location: Right now they are living right near their shuls and schools and near the shopping and a great pizza store. The new house doesn't have such great neighbors…yet.

Repairs: The superintendent takes care of anything in the apartment that breaks. In the ramshackle "new" house, no one is sponsoring the repairs – and there are lots of repairs to be made.

Space: Three bedrooms, one bathroom with three kids is getting a little tight. The new house has four bedrooms, with an alcove that can be used as a study/playroom, an extra bathroom, a bigger living room/dining room and a semi-finished basement that "has potential." There is also a nice-sized backyard.

Financing: The bank will give them a mortgage of up to $235,000, which is 70% of the property value. They have an inheritance of $75,000 from their grandparents. They can borrow $25,000 from relatives and friends to complete the $100,000 down payment.

Payments: Presently, they are paying $1200 in rent. A 15-year mortgage of $235,000 at 5.5% interest will cost them $1900/month, and a 30-year mortgage at 6% (interest rates are usually higher on a longer-term mortgage) will cost them $1400/month. They can manage the 30-year mortgage on their current income, if they squeeze their budget. To be able to afford the 15-year mortgage, Motti or Dini will have to find an additional source of income, but it will take only 15 years for the house to be theirs. They will also have to repay $500/month in private loans for the next four years, which will require them to pay a total of $1900 or $2400/month, depending which mortgage they take – a significant increase over the $1200 rent they are currently paying.

Possible Solution

Motti and Dini decide to go for the 30-year mortgage, and put any extra money they have into their mortgage so that they can pay it off sooner. They can afford the $1400 mortgage, but they need money to pay off the private loans. They decide to buy the house and rent it out. Because the house is a little bit "out," they can get only about $1800/month in rent for it. If they can manage in their current location for another four years, the $1800 in rent will pay their own rent ($1200) plus their private loans ($500), with some allowance for repairs that their tenants will need ($100), while they pay an additional $1400/month for the mortgage. They are also hoping that they will be able to raise the rent on their house, as the neighborhood grows and their location becomes more desirable. Once the private loans are repaid, they can reevaluate.

Alternate Solution

The above solution is one of many possible solutions. Can you come up with an alternate solution to the Hirsch's housing dilemma? Address the above considerations (location, repairs, space, financing, payments) in your solution. Are there any other considerations you think they should take into account? (1 page)

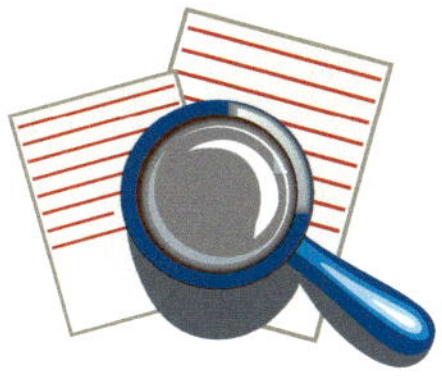

Assignment #5:

Final Course Assignment
Personal Finance Portfolio & Reflection Exercise

Directions:

Part 1. Portfolio

Select the four written items you have prepared during this course that best exhibit your skills, achievements, and efforts within the course. Present this collection of your work as a portfolio showcasing what you have learned.

Part 2. Reflection and Evaluation Exercise

Describe in essay format (1-2 pages) what you have gained in this course. Use the questions below to guide your reflection (addressing at least four of the questions raised).

1. Which specific point raised in the course was most interesting or surprising to you? Why?
2. What part of this course was the least interesting or relevant to you? Why?
3. What are three things that you will do differently in your own financial life as a result of this class?
4. Which ideas covered in the course will be the hardest for you to implement? How do you intend to overcome those difficulties?
5. "Financial mismanagement can magnify or contribute to virtually any other problem."

   Explain this statement, giving specific examples to support it.
6. What personal finance advice or guidelines might you give to a friend based on what you have learned in this course? (Your advice should relate to a specific issue in personal finance, such as credit card use, taking loans, or career choices.)
7. How can the skills encouraged or strengthened in this course (such as prioritizing, decision-making, setting goals, accountability, resourcefulness, and delaying gratification) be applied to other areas of your life?
8. Have you shared anything you've learned in this class with parents, siblings or friends?

   Please elaborate.

The Mesila Student Guide to Budgeting

The Mesila Student Guide to Budgeting

The Mesila Guide to Budgeting

Questions or comments may be sent to:

Mesila USA
POB 838 Monsey NY 10952
Tel: 212.784.6780
info@mesilausa.org
www.mesilausa.org

Table of Contents

A Note to the Student

Dear Student,

Life is not about money, but it sure gets messy when your finances are not in order or you can't live within your means. In theory, living within your means is very simple: spend less than you earn, and you'll be OK!

The problem is that we all have limited money at our disposal, yet there are unlimited possibilities as to what we can do with that money. So the challenge is to use our money in the way that will bring us the maximum benefit and cause us the least financial stress.

Facing this challenge successfully requires a proactive approach: namely, a budget plan. Most people don't like the word budget. It makes them break out into a sweat and think of lots of good reasons why now is not a good time to start budgeting, or why it's not necessary to have a budget.

The reason why budgeting seems so scary is because we tend to associate budgeting with restrictions, deprivation, and stress. People think, *If I have a budget, I'm not going to be able to buy what I want*, or, *If I start budgeting, I'm going to have to worry about how to make my finances work, and they just don't!*

But the truth is that budgeting is not about restrictions at all; it's about giving you **control** over your finances and **freedom** to use your money as you see fit. Your budget doesn't tell you how to spend your money – *you tell your budget how you want to spend your money*. Then your budget helps you to manage your finances in a way that will enable you to spend money on the things you really want.

You might be thinking: Why do I need to learn about this now? I don't have a budget! I don't have finances! I'm only in high school! But surprise, surprise! Now is the perfect time in your life to practice, precisely *because* you don't really have to be responsible for a family budget, which is a really complicated thing, and something that's tough to learn on the job.

Financial management is a very individual thing, and one that every family will approach differently. Nevertheless, having a budget is an important component of financial management **for everyone**. Some people's budgets are so detailed that they leave nothing to chance, and other people's budgets are only basic outlines, but every family needs to have some sort of budget plan in order to stay in – or get back into – the black. When we don't have a plan, we spend more than we can afford without even noticing, and we lose control over our wallets. But with a budget in hand, we regain control of our wallets. And that's a great feeling.

In this guide, you'll learn how to build an effective budget and cash flow plan, and how to avoid common budgeting pitfalls. To make budgeting as simple and straightforward as possible, the step-by-step instructions in the guide are written in clear, easy-to-understand language and are accompanied by frequently asked questions and section summaries.

If you're looking to strike it rich, this program is not for you. But if you're looking for a way to avoid the mistakes that others have made, and control your money instead of letting your money control you, then we hope you'll find this booklet helpful – now, and in the future *b'ezras Hashem*.

Mesila

The First Step: Establish Needs and Wants

Our goal in budgeting is to allow you to have *everything you need and some of what you want*. That means that you have to know the difference between what you need and what you want. It also means that you have to make sure FIRST that you have what you need, and only THEN see if you can have what you want.

Needs and wants are different for different people. Just because your friend, or your neighbor, or even your older sister *needs* something doesn't mean that you do. And just because they *don't need* something doesn't mean that you don't. That's why you have to get to know yourself, your needs, and your wants.

The purpose of the "Track What You Spend" exercise on the following page is:

1. To take note of spending habits so that we can get to know ourselves and how we spend.
2. To differentiate between needs and wants so that we can prioritize.

Other lessons to be learned from tracking what you spend:

1. For every outlay there must be a corresponding source of money. (Making that connection may be the most fundamental principle of financial stability.)
2. Becoming aware of your spending habits enables you to identify unhealthy patterns (or patterns that might become problematic later). **Awareness is the basis of all change.**

The Million Dollar Question

(Reprinted from Mirrors & Windows, by Malky Feig, with the permission of the Publisher. Mesorah Publications, 2005)

I was married two weeks
She, two months, an old pro.
We were discussing the financial issue,
two sages on the matter.
I said something
about newlyweds being stingy,
And she shook her head
waved her hand,
dismissed the idea.
"My husband says" –
she began importantly,
"There's no need to be stingy,
The golden rule is this:
You can buy whatever's necessary.
Just leave out the extras."
I was duly impressed
by her husband's wisdom.
Repeated the rule
to whomever was ready to listen.
I tried implementing it
in my own home,
Until I hit the catch –
The million-dollar question,
which I haven't quite figured out yet.
The rule is bliss,
It solves everything but this:
What are the necessities,
and what are the extras?

Track What You Spend!

Date: From_____________ to ________________

Purchase	Cost	Source of money	Need or Want?

Let's Get Honest.

(Discussion – in class, or with yourself)

1. How do you define "need"?
2. How do you define "want"?
3. Do the things you want bring you lasting benefit?
4. Which purchases do you regret a week later? Why do you have regrets?

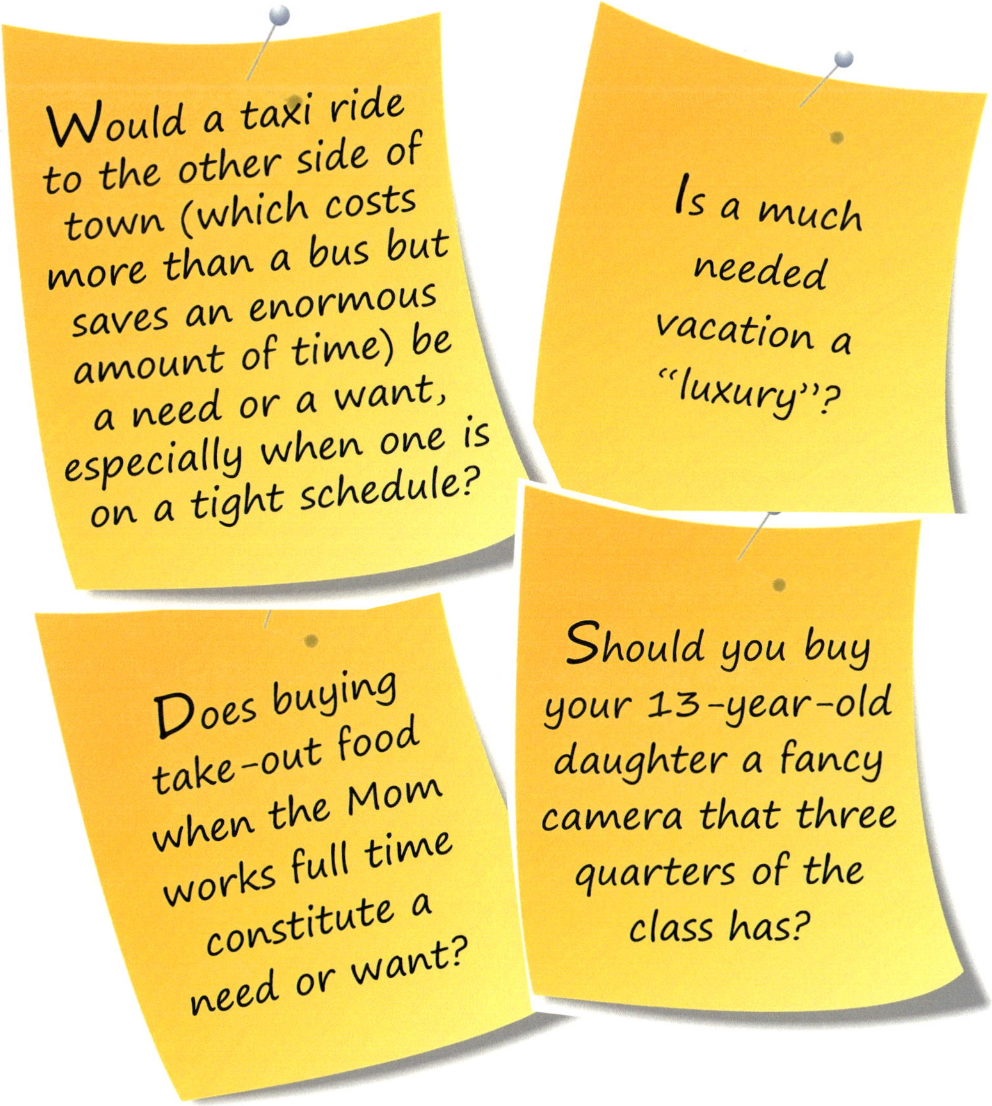

*When does a **want** become a **need**?*
There are no easy answers!

Let's Build a Family Budget

Here are some straightforward steps for creating a workable budget for a family. In other words: If you were trying to create a budget for your family – and b'ezras Hashem you will, one day – this is what you would do.

Step 1:

Determine the family's income

Start by adding up the family's net annual earnings, including:

- Monthly salary and wages (multiplied by twelve)
- Money from side jobs
- Investment earnings
- Interest and dividends
- Government allowances

If the family has any other sources of income (royalties, rent, parental support, etc.), include those as well.

A word of caution: Do not include possible windfalls – such as gifts or year-end bonuses – in your annual income projection.

If a person has bitachon (faith) that Hashem will provide for him, does he still have to budget?

Mesila actually posed this question to Hagaon R' Aaron Leib Steinman. R' Steinman replied, "If a person would go into a forest without water or food and then collapse, would that be *bitachon*? It would be suicide! Similarly, every person needs to live with a budget and calculate his income and expenses."

Budgeting and *bitachon* are not mutually exclusive. Even a person who has *bitachon* needs to budget, and even a person who budgets needs to have *bitachon*!

Step 2:

Track the family's expenses

To track expenses, write down every dollar the family spends for a minimum of 2-3 months. During this time, hold onto all documentation of the family's financial transactions, including:

- Bills
- Invoices
- Bank statements
- Credit card statements
- Cash register receipts

To keep track of expenses as they occur, keep a paper hanging in a conspicuous place – such as on the refrigerator – to remind you to record your expenses as they happen. Alternatively, you may want to carry a little notebook with you so that you can write down expenses as they occur. If you find it difficult to record expenses on an ongoing basis, you can take a few moments at the end of each day to record all of the day's expenses.

In addition to recording each purchase you make, you need to think about all of the other silent ways that money leaks out of your budget, such as:

- Bank and credit card charges
- Automatic bank account withdrawals
- Post-dated checks
- *Tzedakah* contributions
- Items you buy with pocket change

Pay attention to how often you spend small amounts – under $5. **These invisible or seemingly trivial expenses are often responsible for the discrepancy between what you think you spend and what you actually spend.**

Tracking your expenses might be difficult at first, but once you get used to doing it, it will become much easier – and you'll see the benefits very quickly! You'll be amazed at how your increased awareness will put you more in control of your money and help you make smarter spending decisions.

"Yikes! Where did all my money go?"

Has this ever happened to you? You take out your wallet, sure that it's going to be full – but it's empty! *Where did all the money go?* you wonder.

Keeping track of the small stuff is not only for your parents – it can do wonders for your own finances as well. Trivial purchases add up: $2 here, $5 here, and before you know it, that $100 your grandparents gave you is gone.

Try getting into the habit of jotting down what you spend so that you can gain control over your money and use your money in a way that you'll REALLY enjoy.

Should I be tracking all of my financial transactions on a regular basis?

At times, it is necessary to track financial transactions on a daily, item-by-item basis, such as when trying to create a budget and cash flow plan, or when faced with a large, one-time expense (such as a *simchah* or a home renovation). In addition, it is important to track all financial transactions for several months after implementing your budget and cash flow plan, until you are sure that you are successfully following the plan.

Even at other times, you still need to track your financial transactions on a general level to ensure that you are remaining within your budget. But it is not necessary to record every single transaction at that point; reviewing your bank and credit card statements and your check register should give you a pretty good picture of whether you are staying within budget.

If you find it liberating to record all of your financial transactions, since it gives you a sense of control over your money, then by all means, track every transaction. But if tracking your financial transactions down to the last penny makes you feel stifled, then do this detailed tracking only when absolutely necessary. The rest of the time, you can monitor your financial transactions on a more general level.

Step 3:

Calculate the family's expenses

After you have tracked the family's income and expenses for several months, you need to organize the data and group the different income and expense items into general categories. (For instance, group together related expenses such as "taxi ride," "bus card," and "train fare" under a general heading called "transportation.")

Expense categories can be divided into three major groups:

1. Fixed monthly expenses
2. Fluctuating monthly expenses
3. Annual or periodic expenses

Note: When calculating expenses, do not include debt payments (besides the mortgage).

Fixed monthly expenses may include things like:

- Mortgage or rent
- Insurance (life, health, home, auto, etc.)
- Car payments
- Childcare
- Savings plans
- Domestic help

There should be no need for guesswork here, since the amount you pay is usually the same every month.

Fluctuating monthly expenses are a bit trickier. Examples are:

- Food
- Utilities (telephone, cellular phone, electricity, water, gas, etc.)
- Gasoline
- Household products (toiletries, cleaning products, paper goods, etc.)
- Medications
- *Tzedakah* contributions
- Bank charges
- Dry cleaning

These expenses can vary significantly from month to month.

After tracking your expenses for 2-3 months, you should be able to determine a range for these fluctuating expenses. The numbers you will use in your budget should be the ones at the higher end of the range. For instance, if your food bill was $500 one month, $700 the next month, and $400 the next month, you might use $600 as a higher-end estimate of your monthly food costs.

All monthly expenses should be recorded under the month they were incurred, not the date they were paid. For example, if a pipe burst in your house on January 31 and you paid your plumber with a check dated February 28, record the cost of the repair under January's expenses.

Annual and periodic expenses are things like:

- Summer camp
- Medical and dental costs
- Clothing
- Shoes
- Vacations and outings
- *Simchas* and parties
- Home repairs
- Car maintenance
- Travel
- Yom Tov expenses
- Furniture and appliances

Estimate these costs to the best of your ability, using previous years' expenses as a guide.

To determine your total annual expenditure, add up your fixed and fluctuating monthly expenses and multiply the total by twelve. Then add to that your annual or periodic expenses.

Now that you have a fairly accurate estimate of your annual expenditure, pad this figure by 5-10% to allow room for unanticipated expenses. This will give your budget the flexibility to accommodate surprise expenses like parking tickets, lost knapsacks or passport renewals.

After you decide which items belong in which category, we recommend that you ask an objective person outside your immediate family – such as a friend, a neighbor, or a Mesila counselor – to review the items in each category and tell you whether your classifications seem reasonable. This will help you to discover any errors you have made, and may give you ideas for managing your money more effectively. Different families have different spending habits, and there is a lot you can learn a lot from comparing your family's spending habits with those of others.

Mesila's monthly and annual budgeting forms are designed to help you categorize your expenses in an orderly, logical fashion and show you where exactly your money is going.

Step 4:

Compare your income and expenses

Once you have determined how much you are actually spending on a monthly and annual basis, and you have tracked where all the money is going, you can measure your expenses against your income and determine your annual balance using the following formula:

Annual income – Annual expenses = Annual balance

Now that you know what your annual balance is, you can congratulate yourself on having achieved financial awareness. **Awareness is the foundation for all improvement,** since you cannot fix something if you don't know what is wrong with it. If you and your spouse are aware of exactly what your financial situation is, you will be motivated to take the initiative to do whatever you can to improve it. Therefore, achieving awareness is the critical first step in gaining control of your finances, and is the basis for successful budgeting.

Why do I need to know what my annual balance is?

Your annual balance is *the* most important piece of budgetary information you have. Basically, it tells you whether your income exceeds your expenses, or the reverse.

If your annual balance is positive (which means that your income exceeds your expenses), that is the ideal situation: a surplus. You have extra money to save or use as you see fit, and you do not have the pressure of having to change your lifestyle. You may, however, choose to streamline your budget by "trimming the fat" and eliminating or reducing non-essential expenses. This will give you even more financial leverage and will allow you to put your money to the best possible use.

If your annual balance is negative (which means that your income is less than your expenses), you are running a deficit. Governments have the luxury of operating with a deficit; you do not. Even a small monthly deficit, when accumulated, can easily spiral into out-of-control debt. You therefore have to find additional sources of income and/or think of ways to cut down your expenses.

If your annual balance is zero (which means that your income and expenses are equal), then your budget is exactly balanced. Although on the surface, a perfectly balanced budget seems to be an acceptable situation, it is actually not acceptable, for several reasons:

1. It is almost impossible to calculate *all* of your expenses, so your expenses are probably 10-20% higher than you think. Therefore, if your budget is exactly balanced, you are probably running at least a small deficit.

2. A budget that is exactly balanced leaves you no leeway for unanticipated expenses – and there are *always* unanticipated expenses.

3. If your income and expenses are equal, then you have no possibility of saving for the future (or repaying debts, if you have any). Savings are an integral part of any budget, for they empower you to cope with financial challenges in the future and prevent those challenges from becoming crises. And it goes without saying that if you are in debt, it is critical that your budget be configured in a way that will enable you to repay your debts.

Step 5:

Build your budget plan

Now, you can go on to build a budget plan for the future, taking into account both your current income and spending information as well as future income and spending projections. How you will go about building your budget plans depends very much on whether your annual balance is positive or negative (an annual balance of zero is considered a negative balance, for our purposes).

When building your budget plan, it is critical to ensure that you have a significantly positive annual balance. If your annual balance is negative, or if you already have a positive annual balance but you wish to increase it, you will need to find ways to increase your income or reduce your expenses. The budget forms that you filled out earlier will play a vital role in helping you decide what budgetary changes to make.

Now, take a fresh set of monthly and annual budget forms and fill in projected future amounts for each item, based on the data you have collected and any budgetary changes you have decided to implement (i.e., increases in income and reductions in spending). Also include in your new budget any one-time earnings or expenses that you anticipate in the upcoming months. The projections you write down in this fresh set of forms will become your new budget plan.

Once you have successfully built a budget plan, you can go on to create a cash flow plan that will make your budget plan work for you.

Here are some general suggestions for **increasing income:**

- Learn new, marketable skills.
- Upgrade your professional abilities to make yourself more valuable to your employer and earn a promotion or raise.
- Turn a hobby into an income-generating activity.
- Give private or group lessons to teach a subject or skill that you are good at.
- Work additional hours (possibly off-times, such as evenings or weekends).
- Take on side work in addition to your regular occupation.

Here are some general suggestions for **reducing expenses:**

- Use cash exclusively.
- Look for cheaper service providers in all areas – from your phone company to your cleaning help to your dentist.
- Make a shopping list before you buy groceries, including quantities of each item.
- Don't go shopping when you're hungry, in a rush, or feeling down.
- Buy cheaper generic brands instead of brand names.
- Find creative, low-cost alternatives to expensive family outings.

I want to turn my negative annual balance into a positive balance. How do I decide what budgetary changes to make?

Now that your income and expenses are neatly itemized in the monthly and annual budget forms, you should review each income item and decide whether it can be increased; look for ways to bring in income from new sources; and review each expense item and decide whether it can be reduced or removed. Don't be embarrassed to ask others for their advice when deciding what budgetary changes to make.

But be realistic when making these decisions. Try not to make drastic or sweeping budget cuts, since these typically cause severe stress in the home and are rarely sustainable long-term. Small, localized cuts are usually less painful and more easily implemented.

In general, increasing income is a better way to improve your annual balance than cutting expenses, since the potential for increasing income is theoretically unlimited, and increasing income may involve less stress. It is difficult to plan a budget based on possible increases in income, though, so be very careful when inflating your income projections for the future.

The process of making changes to your current budget often involves much trial and error, so do not be discouraged if your planned budget cuts or hoped-for increases in income do not materialize as you would have liked. If your first attempts at improving your annual balance don't work out the way you would like, keep on trying! You'll get there, with Hashem's help.

Monthly Budget

(Current/Projected)

A. Monthly Income

	Source: Salary/Wages (net)	Amount		Source: Interest/Dividends	Amount	Other Sources	Amount	Other Sources	Amount
Husband			Investment type			Rent			
						Child benefits			
						Unemployment benefits			
Wife						Social Security / Social Insurance			
						Pension/Retirement Fund			

Total Monthly Income

$

B. Monthly Expenses*

Expense Category	Amount	% of Total Expenditure
1: Housing		
2: Food & Household Items		
3: Bills & Utilities		
4: Education & Children		
5: Transportation		
6: Health & Personal Care		
7: Leisure		
8: Miscellaneous		

* See itemized list of expenses on next page.

Space for Calculations

Total Monthly Expenses

$

C. Monthly Balance

Total Monthly Income (end of section A)		Total Monthly Expenses (end of section B)		circle		Monthly Balance
$	−	$	=	+ / −	»	$

Itemized List of Expenses for Section B of Monthly Budget

Item 1: Housing	
Rent	
Mortgage	
Property tax	
Building dues	
Cleaning help	
Outdoor maintenance	
Other	
Total:	

Item 2: Food & Household Items	
Meat & fish	
Fruits & vegetables	
Bread & baked goods	
Packaged foods	
Beverages	
Snack foods	
Restaurant & takeout	
Health food	
Household items	
Paper goods	
Cleaning supplies	
Other	
Total:	

Item 3: Bills & Utilities	
Social Security / Social Insurance	
Telephone	
Cell phone	
Electricity	
Gas / Heating oil	
Water	
Life insurance	
Appliance service contracts	
Bank charges	
Credit card charges	
Interest charges	
Other	
Total:	

Item 4: Education & Children	
School tuition / playgroup	
Daycare	
School transportation	
Babysitting	
Private lessons	
Tutoring	
Baby items	
Pocket money	
Support for single children	
Support for married children	
Other	
Total:	

Item 5: Transportation	
Auto lease	
Gasoline	
Tolls	
Buses	
Taxis	
Carpool	
Other	
Total:	

Item 6: Health & Personal Care	
Health insurance	
Medicines	
Vitamins	
Fitness	
Therapies	
Alternative medicine	
Contact lenses & solutions	
Toiletries & cosmetics	
Health & beauty treatments	
Haircuts	
Other	
Total:	

Item 7: Leisure	
Newspapers & magazines	
Gifts	
Flowers	
Stationery & crafts	
Lottery & raffle tickets	
Entertainment	
Other	
Total:	

Item 8: Miscellaneous	
Tzedakah	
Support for parents	
Savings plan	
Dry cleaning	
Pet expenses	
Other	
Total:	

Annual Budget

(Current/Projected)

D. Periodic Income

Periodic Income	Amount	Comments
Year-end bonus		
Tax refund		
Government benefits		
Charitable assistance		
Gifts		

Reduction of Income	Amount	Comments
Nissan		
Summer		
Tishrei		

Periodic Income		Reduction of Income		Total Periodic Income
$	−	$	= ›	$

E. Periodic Expenses*

Expense Category	Amount	% of Total Expenditure
1: Housing		
2: Clothing		
3: Education & Children		
4: Transportation		
5: Health & Personal Care		
6: *Yomim Tovim*		
7: Leisure		
8: Miscellaneous		

* See itemized list of expenses on next page. Record only those expenses that are not included in your monthly budget.

Space for Calculations

Total Periodic Expenses

› $

F. Periodic Balance

Total Periodic Income (end of section D)		Total Periodic Expenses (end of section E)		circle	Periodic Balance
› $	−	› $	= ››	+ −	$

G. Annual Balance

Monthly Balance (end of section C on Monthly Budget)

› $ × 12 › $

+ Periodic Balance (end of section F) › $

= ››› circle + − Annual Balance $

÷12 circle + − Adjusted Monthly Balance $

Itemized List of Expenses for Section E of Annual Budget

Item 1: Housing	
Homeowner's insurance	
Heating oil/gas	
Home repairs	
Appliance purchases	
Appliance repairs	
Furniture	
Lighting	
Kitchen supplies	
Pest control	
Other	
Total:	
Item 2: Clothing	
Clothing – parents	
Clothing – children	
Shoes – parents	
Shoes – children	
Jewelry & accessories	
Outerwear	
Head coverings	
Shaitel care	
Other	
Total:	
Item 3: Education & Children	
Enrichment for children	
Courses & *shiurim*	
School activities & other costs	
School supplies	
Summer camp	
Day camp	
Other	
Total:	
Item 4: Transportation	
Car insurance	
Car inspection & licensing	
Car repair & maintenance	
Emissions testing	

Parking & tickets	
Shipping	
Postage	
Other	
Total:	
Item 5: Health & Personal Care	
Medical expenses	
Medical equipment	
Dental & orthodontic	
Glasses	
Contact lenses	
Other	
Total:	
Item 6: *Yamim Tovim*	
Tishrei:	
Arba minim	
Succah	
Shul seats	
Yom Tov food	
Clothing & shoes	
Chol Hamoed outings	
Other	
Total - Tishrei:	
Purim:	
Mishloach Manot	
Matanot L'evyonim	
Costumes	
Gifts	
Other	
Total – Purim:	
Pesach:	
Matzah	
Yom Tov food – general	
Wine	
Fruits & vegetables	
Meat & fish	
Cleaning help & supplies	

Dishes & utensils	
Clothing & shoes	
Chol Hamoed outings	
Afikoman presents	
Other	
Total – Pesach:	
Shavuos	
Chanukah	
Tu b'Shevat	
Other	
- Total **:all *Yamim Tovim***	
Item 7: Leisure	
Vacations	
Summer residence	
Recreation	
Electronics	
Sports & hobbies	
Toys & games	
Music	
Gifts	
Photography	
Simchas & parties	
Other	
Total:	
Item 8: Miscellaneous	
Tzedakah	
Shul dues	
Aliyos	
Seforim & books	
Computer equipment	
Personal article insurance	
Government documentation	
Other	
Total:	

The Next Frontier: Building a Cash Flow Plan

To keep your finances under control, it's not enough to build a budget. You also need to prepare a cash flow plan. A cash flow plan is simply a way of ensuring that you'll have the money you need, when you need it.

Why is this necessary? Because expenses – and in some cases, income – fluctuate from month to month. Even if your annual budget is balanced and you are earning enough money over the year to cover all of your expenses, you may still find yourself short on cash during peak-expense seasons such as Yamim Tovim or summer vacation.

A cash flow plan will help to ensure that when these peak-expense seasons arrive, you have enough money on hand to cover your bills. It will also help you to determine how much money you need to set aside during low-expense months to carry you through higher-expense months.

For people who do not earn regular monthly salaries, a cash flow plan is even more critical. A real estate agent might earn $10,000 in commissions one month, but nothing for the next two months. A freelancer who does not receive employee benefits might bring home a respectable income during months that have twenty-plus work days, but very little during months that include numerous sick or vacation days. A clothing store owner might post impressive revenues at the beginning of the winter and summer seasons, but have pitifully low mid-season sales. To make matters worse, peak-income seasons do not always coincide with peak-expense seasons; in fact, many self-employed people experience a significant drop in income during peak-expense seasons. (For instance, a musician may not have much work during the Three Weeks, but he still has to pay for his children's summer camp...)

Often, people whose income fluctuates exhibit a "feast/famine" lifestyle pattern, in which they live well during peak-income months, and experience severe financial strain during months when income slows to a trickle. This is extremely stressful, and quite avoidable. To ride out the peaks and troughs of irregular income, you need to develop a cash flow plan that will help you spread your income across the year.

Now that we've discussed budgeting, we will go on to an explanation of how to use your budget as a basis for a cash flow plan.

How do I build a cash flow plan?

When planning your budget, you made proactive decisions as to how you want to spend your money, within the boundaries created by your income. Now that you have a balanced budget, you also have to make sure that you will have enough money on hand to pay for the items included in your budget in a timely manner.

Don't rely on your wallet, or your bank account, to tell you what you can or can't afford. If you listen to your wallet instead of your budget, you're likely to spend money frivolously when your wallet is full and be overly tightfisted when your wallet is empty.

How do you make sure that your wallet is working in tandem with your budget, so that you have the right amount of money at the right time? That's the job of your cash flow plan.

The form entitled "Cash Flow Plan" is designed to help you calculate your projected cash flow and make any necessary adjustments.

In order to build a cash flow plan, you will need to calculate approximately how much money will be coming in (positive cash flow) and how much money will be going out (negative cash flow) during each of the next twelve months.

It is important to realize that **positive cash flow is not synonymous with income, and negative cash flow is not synonymous with expenses**. A person can have lots of income, and yet have negative cash flow – for instance, if his wages are delayed or if his money is tied up in investments and therefore inaccessible. Conversely, a person can have little or no income, and yet have positive cash flow – for instance, if he borrows money or liquidates his assets. (Keep in mind, however, that borrowed money quickly turns into negative cash flow when the time comes to repay it…)

Examples of positive cash flow items: +

- Income that is *paid* (not owed) to you
- Monetary gifts
- Revenue from the liquidation of assets
- Money that you borrow

Examples of negative cash flow items: –

- All purchases and payments
- Automated withdrawals from your bank account
- Money you put in savings or investments
- Debt repayments

Here is a step-by-step guide to building your cash flow plan:

Step 1:

Estimate the timing of annual income and expenses

When you built your budget plan, you differentiated between *monthly* income and expenses and *annual* (or *periodic*) income and expenses. Now, go through your itemized list of annual income and expenses and try to determine in which month each income or expense item belongs. The timing of certain annual budget items (such as holiday expenses, or summer camp) is easy to predict, while other items are difficult or impossible to predict; you do not know, for instance, when you might need to pay for a home repair. Annual budget items whose timing is predictable should be entered on the form under the month in which they are likely to happen.All other annual income and expenses should be added up separately and recorded as "remainder."

Step 2:

Estimate all other projected cash flow for each month

To estimate your projected cash flow for each month, you need to account for all projected positive and negative cash flow during that month. Your cash flow projections for any given month should include:

- Your regular monthly income and expenses
- The portion of your annual income and expenses that you anticipate during that month (which you calculated in step 1 above)
- Any other money that might be coming in or going out during that month (including a portion of your annual remainder, if applicable – see next paragraph).

The remainder you calculated in step one, representing the sum of all annual budget items whose timing is unpredictable, has to be assigned to the various months of the year. You can do this by dividing the total remainder by 12 and adding that figure (one-twelfth of the total remainder) to each month's cash flow figures. Alternatively, you can assign the remainder of your annual expenses to the first two or three months of the year and the remainder of your annual income to the last two or three months to ensure that you are prepared for unpredictable expenses whenever they happen. This money should be put aside in a place that is readily accessible, but not *too* accessible, to ensure that you are not tempted to use it for other purposes.

Obviously, your cash flow estimates will be far from perfect. Unpredictable annual expenses might all happen in the beginning of the year; they might all happen at the end of the year; or they might happen at various times throughout the year. They certainly won't cooperate with your cash flow plan and divide themselves evenly over the twelve months of the year. **Because you have no way of knowing when these expenses will**

happen, the best you can do is give a reasonable estimate. It is therefore important that you monitor your actual cash flow throughout the year and make any necessary midcourse corrections.

Step 3:

Calculate your projected monthly cash flow balance

Once you have those estimates, the next step is to calculate your projected cash flow balance for each of the next twelve months, using the following formula:

Total positive cash flow
– Total negative cash flow
= Cash flow balance

A positive balance in a particular month means that you will have a surplus during that month; a negative balance means that you will have a deficit during that month.

You now have a cash flow projection for the next twelve months.

Step 4:

Make adjustments for negative cash flow periods

Based on your cash flow projection, you can go on to make adjustments to compensate for the period(s) in which you anticipate a negative cash flow.

Adjusting for negative cash flow means finding a source from which to finance the deficit you are anticipating during a given period. If the period in which you anticipate negative cash flow comes after a period of positive cash flow, the best thing to do is to put aside money during the positive cash flow period to tide you over the negative cash flow period. But if the negative cash flow period comes first, or if you are unable to put aside enough money during the positive cash flow period to tide you through the negative cash flow period, then you will need to find an alternate financing source. This source can be either internal (liquidating your own savings, investments, or assets) or external (taking interim loans or credit). In most cases, tapping into your own resources is preferable to borrowing from an external source.

Does it matter whether I start my cash flow plan in a positive cash flow month or a negative cash flow month?

A cash flow plan is meant to empower you to ride out the budgetary fluctuations that inevitably occur throughout the year. Therefore, it is worthwhile to begin a cash flow plan in a position of strength, with cash in hand to tide you through the negative cash flow period ahead, rather than begin the plan with a deficit and constantly have to look back and cover past expenses.

If it is not possible to jumpstart the cash flow plan with cash in hand, however, then it is important to plan *how much* money you will need to cover your negative cash flow, *where* you will take it from, and *how* and *when* you will pay it back. Planning cash flow financing carefully will enable you to borrow or withdraw only the amount you actually need, and ensure that you have a way to repay the loan or replenish your resources.

Cash Flow Plan

A. Projected Annual/Periodic Expenses by Month

In section E of the Annual Budget, you entered totals for each of the eight periodic expense categories listed. Now, calculate what portion of those periodic expense categories can be assigned to specific months and record the amounts below. The portion of the periodic expense categories that is unpredictable should be recorded under "Remainder."

For instance: Most purchases in the clothing category typically take place at the beginning of the winter and summer seasons, so you might assign 40% of your clothing budget to the month of September and 40% to the month of April, and then record the remaining 20% under "Remainder," since you don't know in which month you will incur the remaining clothing expenses.

Month	Projected Expense: Category 1 - Housing	Projected Expense: Category 2 - Clothing	Projected Expense: Category 3 - Education & Children	Projected Expense: Category 4 - Transportation	Projected Expense: Category 5 - Health & Personal Care	Projected Expense: Category 6 - Holidays	Projected Expense: Category 7 - Leisure	Projected Expense: Category 8 - Miscellaneous	Total Projected Expenses: All categories
Month 1									
Month 2									
Month 3									
Month 4									
Month 5									
Month 6									
Month 7									
Month 8									
Month 9									
Month 10									
Month 11									
Month 12									
Total									
Grand Total*									
Remainder (Grand total - Total)									

* Take these figures from section E of Annual Budget.

This is the sum of the projected expense amounts listed above for the 12 months of the year.

Flip back to Section E of the Annual Budget, and transfer to this row the figures listed in the eight categories of the Amount column.

This figure shows the portion of each periodic expense category that is unpredictable. You can't know exactly when these expenses will crop up.

B. Cash Position by Month

In this table, enter monthly estimates for each of the positive and negative cash flow categories and calculate the monthly balance. If the monthly balance is negative, indicate how you plan to cover the deficit by recording the proposed adjustment source and amount.

	Positive cash flow				Negative cash flow								
Month	Projected Monthly Income	Projected Annual/ Periodic Income	Remainder	Other	Projected Monthly Expenses	Projected Annual/ Periodic Expenses (from Table A above)	Savings Plan	Debt Repay-ment	Remainder	Other	Monthly Balance	Adjustment Source	Adjustment Amount
Month 1													
Month 2													
Month 3													
Month 4													
Month 5													
Month 6													
Month 7													
Month 8													
Month 9													
Month 10													
Month 11													
Month 12													

The Final Challenge:
Divide & Conquer

The following is an article that appeared in Mesila's Hamodia column.

A Tale of Two Incomes — and a Deficit

Question:

Our financial situation was always such that we never were able to make ends meet. For the first few years after we got married, my husband learned in kollel. We lived very frugally then, but we nevertheless got into debt. When my husband began working part-time, we moved to a different community, where our expenses increased, and so did our debt. We were running to gemachim constantly. Eventually, my husband got a full-time job in a brokerage firm with an income that started at about $25,000 a year (this goes back some twenty years). At that time, the income was inadequate to cover our expenses, and we got ourselves into serious credit card debt.

Over the years, our income has increased. I became a dental hygienist several years ago so I bring home about $3,000 a month, which does help a lot. Our total monthly take home income is presently $10,160, plus my husband's year-end bonus of $10,000.

We still owe a lot of back taxes, and we have a monthly arrangement to pay these taxes. But we often end up buying food with post-dated checks, and we still occasionally get shut off notices from the utility companies. Our financial situation has caused my husband major stress and has really affected the atmosphere in our home.

I'm concerned that we may be really mismanaging our money, since considering our income, we should be managing comfortably. When I list the expenses, though, it looks as though we need several thousand dollars a month more.

Our monthly expenses (not including food, groceries, clothing, yom tov costs, gifts, etc.) are $9,346, itemized below:

Mortgage:	*$2,250*
Property taxes:	*$700*
Gas and electric:	*$600*
Water:	*$80*
Cleaners:	*$120*
Tuition for two children:	*$1,050*
School transportation:	*$230*
Allowance for son learning in Israel:	*$400*
Cleaning help:	*$320*
Pay back on down payment for house:	*$300*
Gemach payments:	*$925*
Income tax (owed from past):	*$350*
Car payments:	*$516*
Car insurance:	*$300*
Gasoline:	*$350*
Homeowners' insurance:	*$125*
Credit card debt (old):	*$250*
Credit card payments:	*$120 (just interest)*
Medicine:	*$100*
Telephone:	*$100*
Cell phones (3):	*$160*

Any help or advice that you can offer would be greatly appreciated.

Mesila's response:

We welcome your inquiry, and we will be happy to assist you to the best of our ability. The situation you describe is all too common, particularly in the U.S.: two parents working hard to earn a respectable combined income, yet struggling to meet their financial obligations.

Mesila's counseling program involves three stages, the first and most basic of which is helping a family become aware of its exact financial situation. You have done an excellent job coming up with a detailed budget breakdown, and we congratulate you on taking this first step towards financial stability. Because you have provided us with a breakdown of your budget, we can hopefully zero in on the source of the problem and offer some suggestions for solving it.

What seems to be preventing you from achieving financial stability is the fact that about 20% of your income is going towards repayment of old debts – not including your mortgage – so you continually have to borrow money to cover your ongoing living expenses.

The way Mesila recommends that you break this vicious cycle is by separating debt from living expenses, using what we call the "divide and conquer approach." Debts and living expenses have to be viewed as two distinct financial obligations and managed as two separate accounts. Your income is meant to cover your living expenses, and your debts have to be paid for from a separate fund.

In the budget breakdown you sent us, debts are lumped together with living expenses and are not itemized. (For instance, when you say "Gemach payments," how many *gemachim* are you paying and how much do you owe to each of them?) The first thing you need to do, therefore, is create a separate, itemized list of debts.

The second thing you need to do is ensure that your annual income is covering your annual living expenses. You have done a good job of itemizing a portion of your monthly expenses above, but it is crucial that you add food, groceries, clothing, yom tov expenses, gifts, and whatever is included in "etc." to your list so that you can determine how much you are really spending. You also need to account for annual and occasional expenses (such as summer camp, or car and home repairs), so that your figures reflect the true annual picture of your finances, rather than a narrow monthly slice of the yearly expense pie.

Once you have accurate figures of your annual income and expenses, you will be able to calculate your annual balance by subtracting expenses from income. If the balance is positive, then you have an annual budget surplus, and you can move on to build a long-term debt repayment plan. If your balance is zero, slightly more than zero, or negative, then you will have to work on increasing your income and/or decreasing your expenditures so that you can carve out a budget surplus, which will become your debt repayment fund.

Whether your annual balance is positive, negative, or zero, you should never use borrowed money to pay for living expenses. Borrowed money includes post-dated checks, installment plans, buying on credit at local stores, and even credit cards, if you are carrying over a balance from month to month. It is critical that your living expenses be covered by your income, to ensure that your debts do not continue to mount. A family that runs an ongoing monthly deficit is headed for financial disaster, so if you find that your income is not covering your living expenses, then you will have to implement emergency measures – which may include working overtime, implementing spending cuts, or even taking *tzedakah* – to close the gap.

We are hopeful, however, that your living expenses *can* be covered by your income, considering that you are earning a very respectable net income of $10,160 a month. Assuming that this is the case, then once you have calculated your annual budget surplus, you can work on creating a fund for debt repayment. This is done by allocating money for all of your living expenses, and then building a long-term debt repayment plan based on your annual budget surplus, which is the amount you can afford to put towards debt repayment every year.

To illustrate, let's say your annual budget surplus is $10,000. If that is the case, you may decide to repay $833 ($10,000 divided by 12) every month. Or, you may decide that you prefer to repay $1,000 ten times a year, so that you do not have to make debt repayments around the times of Pesach and Succos, when your expenses are higher and your income might be reduced. Either way, your debt will be reduced by $10,000 a year. If you find that you can afford to channel more money into your debt repayment fund as time goes on, that is wonderful, but you have to be very careful that paying extra does not result in financial hardship that will lead you to take on more debts or abandon your debt repayment plan because it is too constricting.

In order to create your debt repayment plan, you will probably have to renegotiate the repayment terms of some of the old debts so that your monthly payments can be tailored to an amount that reflects your annual budget surplus. Another option is to consolidate your debt by taking out one large loan to pay off all of the old debts. If you decide to take out a new loan to consolidate your debt, make sure that (a) the monthly payments do not exceed the amount that can afford to repay and (b) the new loan is exactly equal to the amount you owe. (If it is more than you currently owe, your debt will increase; if it is less than you currently owe, you will still be saddled with the burden of repaying multiple debts.)

The advantage of paying back your debts in this manner is that you are able to eliminate your debts as quickly as you can afford to without having to take on any new debts in the interim and without severely compromising your standard of living.

Please realize, however, that the plan that we have just outlined is purely theoretical. To create a realistic, workable plan, you need to invest time and effort to build the plan. As time goes on, you will also need to continually reevaluate your financial situation and your debt load and fine-tune the plan based on your changing financial realities.

Because building – and following – such a plan is challenging, we strongly recommend that you either find someone whom you trust to act as your financial counselor, or apply for Mesila's assistance.

The road to financial stability is often long and arduous, but you seem to be organized, disciplined and motivated enough to succeed in the journey. Feel free to contact us with any further questions.

As we saw in the above article, *A Tale of Two Incomes – and a Deficit*, a common budgeting pitfall is allowing different elements of your finances to get mixed up. In order to really know what's going on and manage your money correctly, you need to differentiate between the following:

Income: Money **coming in** that belongs to you

Assets: Money or property that you currently own

Liabilities: Money that you owe or property that causes you loss

Expenses: Money that you spend as part of your living costs

Maintaining Order – The Divide-and-Conquer Approach

Distinguishing between the many aspects of your finances – which Mesila calls the "divide-and-conquer approach" – is important for two reasons: it helps you to gain an awareness of exactly what is happening with your money, and it puts you in control of your finances by enabling you to make informed decisions.

To implement the divide-and-conquer approach, you should differentiate assets from ongoing income, and debt from ongoing expenses. Loans cannot be considered income, nor can their repayment be considered a living expense. Managing debts and living expenses as two separate accounts will make it possible to get a clear picture of what is going on in each account, and will allow you to achieve control over both accounts in an efficient, orderly manner.

The divide-and-conquer approach extends to other aspects of your finances as well. One-time sources of income have to be differentiated from ongoing or occasional income, and one-time expenses have to be differentiated from your ongoing budget. This ensures that your estimated monthly or annual income is not artificially inflated by a one-time windfall, and that your estimated monthly or annual expenses are not artificially inflated by a one-time outlay.

Similarly, if you have a business, it has to be treated as a separate account. When business and family finances become mixed together, it becomes impossible to reach awareness of what is happening in either one. Separating business finances from family finances makes it possible to reach awareness of what is happening in both, which in turn allows each of them to be managed effectively.

In summary, Mesila uses the divide-and-conquer approach to differentiate between:

- Monthly, annual, occasional and one-time sources of income
- Income and assets
- Living expenses and debt
- Monthly, annual, occasional and one-time expenses
- Business and family finances

Once you have differentiated between these elements of your finances, you will be able to isolate problematic areas from non-problematic areas. Seeing that you are succeeding in at least some areas of your financial management will give you the confidence and motivation to extend your success to other, more problematic areas.

After identifying the areas of your finances that are in need of improvement, you will be in a position to develop distinct strategies to deal with each of those areas.

Financial problems often seem overwhelming, with no solutions in sight. In Mesila's experience, however, even the most complex problems can become manageable if they are broken down into individual, distinct problems and tackled piece by piece.

Divide & Conquer Exercise

The purpose of the following exercise is:

1. To differentiate between the various elements of a family's finances
2. To learn that income has to be designated first for ongoing living expenses to prevent debt from accumulating. (If you use your income to repay debt, you may have to borrow to pay living expenses.)
3. To learn that assets are intended for future or one-time expenses such as buying a home, making weddings, retirement, etc.

Instructions: Categorize each of the items at the bottom of this page into the four categories of the table below.

Income	Assets	Expenses	Liabilities

Bank charges
Bank overdraft
Birthday money
Bonds
Cash
Certificates of deposits (CDs)
Checking accounts
Commissions
Credit card balance
Credit card fees
Debts
Fellowship grant/stipend
Gifts to others

Grocery account
Home
Income tax
Insurance deductible
IRA/401 (k)/RRSP – Canada
Loans owed to you
Mortgage
Mutual funds
Parental support/allowance
Paycheck
Personal valuables (jewelry, etc.)
Post-dated checks
Properties

Property tax
Rent
Retirement funds
Savings accounts
Stocks/shares
Stock dividends
Student loans
Summer residence
Tax refund
Tuition
Tzedakah
Vacations

I have a budget, a cash flow plan, and I've gotten things organized. Now what?

Now that you have created a workable budget and cash flow plan, you need to continue tracking your cash flow for several months until you are sure that your projections are in line with the reality.

About halfway through each month, you should tally all positive and negative cash flow since the beginning of that month. Compare these numbers to your cash flow projections for the month, and see whether you are on target to stay within your budget. If you notice that you are deviating from your budget, now is the time to make a midcourse correction, either by finding a way to increase your income for the month or by spending less than you had planned for the remainder of the month.

If you find yourself consistently deviating from your budget or cash flow plan – in either direction – that is an indication that your budget needs to be reworked. If you are frequently spending more than your budget allows, you may have to recalculate your expenses and adjust your budget to more accurately reflect your true expenses. If you are frequently spending less than your budget allows, you might want to consider upping the amount you designate for savings.

Once you have successfully followed your budget for several months, and you have seen that your income and expense projections are accurate, you may choose to stop tracking your financial transactions on a daily, item-by-item basis. Nevertheless, you should still keep a basic record of how much money is coming in and how much is going out each month, to ensure that you are remaining within your budget and cash flow plan. In addition, when you are anticipating a costly occasion (such as a wedding, or moving to a new home) or a high-expense season (such as Pesach or summer vacation), you should track each expense associated with that particular occasion or season so that you can determine exactly how much you spent. This will help you plan for future occasions, and will also allow you to separate ongoing expenses from one-time expenses so that you can determine whether you have stayed within your regular budget for ongoing expenses.

After your budget is in place and working well, you and your spouse should schedule regular meetings – monthly, or at least quarterly – to assess whether you have stayed within your budget and, if necessary, adjust your budget to reflect your family's changing circumstances.

Long-term Budgeting

Until now, we have been talking about building a short-term budget, which is basically a one-year financial plan that reflects your current income and expenses and also includes provisions for savings (and debt repayment, if necessary).

Ideally, however, your budget should be composed of two parts: a short-term budget and a long-term budget. A long-term budget is less detailed than a short-term budget, simply because it is not possible to make accurate budgetary predictions for the distant future.

To build a long-term budget, you need to look ahead and consider what major expenses you anticipate during the next few years: Do you have a child who is going to need orthodontic work? Are you planning to renovate your house? Are you hoping to make a wedding?

Your long-term budget should include savings for any large, foreseeable expenses during the next few years, and it should include savings for unforeseeable expenses as well. This way, when you encounter an unexpected financial pitfall – e.g., your car breaks down, or you require a medical procedure that your insurance does not cover – you will be prepared. We have to expect the unexpected, because unexpected expenses happen to everyone. The only things that are unexpected about unexpected expenses is *what* they will be and *when* they will happen – not *whether* they will happen.

Your long-term budget should also include provisions for anticipated increases or decreases in income .And if you are in debt ,your long-term budget must include a realistic strategy for repaying *all* of your debts.

How do I know if my budget is ***workable?***

In order for a budget to work, it has to be realistic and somewhat flexible. If unbudgeted-for expenses continually arise, or if routine expenses consistently exceed their budgeted allotment, those are indications that the budget is too restrictive and needs to be reworked.

A good budget is one that does all of the following:

- Generously covers all essentials
- Leaves some room for non-essentials
- Makes provisions for unanticipated expenses
- Incorporates both short- and long-term savings

This type of budget creates financial structure, takes the focus in the home off money issues and contributes to an environment in which healthy family relationships can flourish.

Living with a budget requires discipline, but it should not make you feel deprived. If you have indeed created a realistic budget, you should be able to acquire all of the things you *need*, and some – but probably not all – of the things you *want*. Nobody has everything they want, but if you build your budget correctly, you'll be able to have the things that are most important to you, and you should not feel that you are missing much by forgoing the things that you have left out of your budget.

Overview:
Steps of Budgeting

The main steps involved in building a budget and cash flow plan are:

1. Determine your total income.
2. Track your expenses for several months.
3. Group expenses into major categories.
4. Calculate your annual budget balance.
5. Decide what budgetary changes you wish to make.
6. Build your budget plan, ensuring that you have a budgetary surplus.
7. Estimate positive and negative cash flow for each of the next 12 months.
8. Calculate your cash flow balance for each of the next 12 months.
9. Make adjustments for negative cash flow periods.
10. Give your budget a test run, tweaking it as necessary.
11. Continually review your budget and adjust it to reflect new realities.
12. Build a long-term budget.

ff family*feature*

Downsize

The Art of Living with Less

upgr

A table, some chairs, a folding cot – our succahs pass the minimalist test with flying colors. And for good reason: one of the themes of the Yom Tov is redefining our relationship with the physical. And the lessons we learn need not vanish once we take down our succahs; downsizing can enrich our lives both physically and emotionally

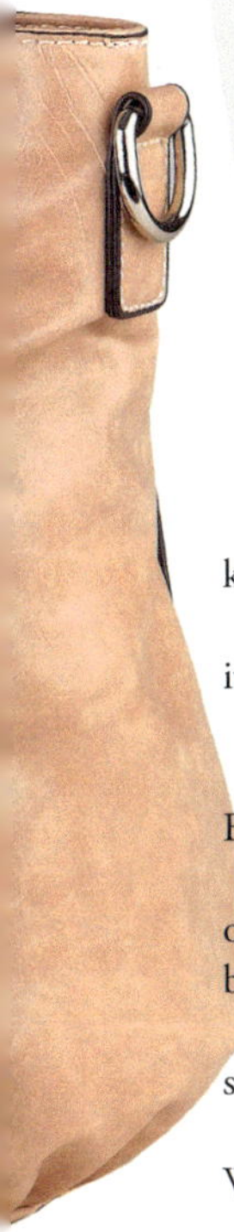

MICHAL EISIKOWITZ

On January 12, 2005, Raizy Weiss's* bedroom fixture exploded. Though firefighters fought hard to contain the flames, she watched from the street corner as an electric fire ravaged the entire second floor of her home.

Traumatized — yet deeply grateful the loss was only material — Raizy numbly set out to build a wardrobe and furniture set from scratch. Once the dust settled and the shock subsided, she made an astonishing discovery: apart from two *sheitels* and a cherished set of her children's baby pictures, she wasn't missing much.

"Virtually nothing destroyed was really valuable to me," she relates. "Most of what was burned, I never used."

Surprising? Not for someone like ardent minimalist Everett Bogue.

"It's like 'What do I actually use in my daily life?' " Everett exclaims while revealing a totally empty cabinet in his stark-would-be-an-understatement kitchen.

A devotee of the "100 Thing Challenge," a group whose members aim to own no more than one hundred items, Everett owns a total of fifty-seven items, including a bed, a couch, and a laptop computer. His raison d'etre is "less is more" — and he's awfully proud of it.

"Two pots, two pans, a pair of shoes," says a smiling Everett as he shows off five of his paltry panoply of possessions.

Readers may be wagging their heads, wondering why yet another nutty fellow is being gloriously wheeled into the spotlight. But statistics show Everett may not be as loopy as you think.

According to the National Association of Professional Organizers, the average person uses only 20 percent of what he owns, and wears 20 percent of his clothing 80 percent of the time. If that's the case, we stuff-lovers might be the fools around here, insisting on cluttering our homes — and our brainspace.

"I began to feel lighter and freer," attests Jenn DiPiazza, a former packrat who embarked on an all-out downsizing campaign after an eye-opening stay in a spartan Navajo reservation. "I was no longer weighed down by all this stuff."

Everett and Jenn are not alone in their quest for simplicity. The "buy no more" mindset is gaining momentum, asserts professional organizer Peter Walsh, due in large part to the recession. While not everybody is downsizing voluntarily, almost everyone is trying to make do with less.

"We're moving to a deeper level of contentment and happiness that's not tied to the accumulation of stuff," says Mr. Walsh.

* *Name has been changed*

Personal downsizing is "in." That's good news for the Jews, since Chazal have long enumerated the virtues of simple living. So while you may not be ready to slash your possessions to the double-digit level, downscaling offers unique benefits that adherents claim have greatly enhanced their quality of life — both physical and spiritual.

WHY DOWNSIZE?

On hearing of the stuff-slimming trend, the first question for many individuals is "why bother?" Downsizing takes time and effort — and emotionally, it's not always a breeze.

But fans of the practice insist that the liberating feeling engendered is worth the price.

"It's a catalyst for freedom," writes "Simply Stephen," a personal downsizing guru. "One can enjoy the things they have more. Cupboards have space. Life has less clutter. It takes less time to maintain everything."

Directing energies towards downsizing can also change personal spending habits: stuff doesn't make you happy anymore.

"An abundant life can be spent *doing* things instead of *acquiring* things," says Stephen.

Mrs. Zlata Press, principal of Brooklyn's Prospect Park Bnos Leah High School, takes this a step further with a thought from the Netziv (*HaEmek Davar*, *Devarim* 4:1): "Materialism stresses the importance of 'things' and devalues the importance of spirit," she paraphrases. "Downsizing, on the other hand, allows one to focus on life's real pleasures."

Still others find that downsizing offers enormous practical benefits: more space, plus the peace of mind knowing the location of each of your possessions.

"It's the *nachas* of a clean, clutter-free desk," muses Edna Deblinger,* a mother and grandmother. Edna — owner of a spacious but furniture-filled home — can't claim to have downsized on the scale she'd like, but she's trying. "Over the years, I've learned that not having to struggle to find what you need each morning is a huge thing."

According to the National Association of Professional Organizers, the average person uses only 20 percent of what he owns, and wears 20 percent of his clothing 80 percent of the time

The case for downsizing becomes even more compelling when you face the facts that most of what we have, we don't use.

Shlomo* came to this realization by accident. Before a move overseas, he got rid of 10 percent of his stuff and stored the rest. When he returned, he realized that most of it wasn't missed.

"I hadn't needed it; it served no purpose," remembers Shlomo, who since became a hard-core downsizer.

Indeed, some individuals discover that the magic of minimalism lies in the economical distribution of resources.

"Our joy comes from the fact that we're not wasting," writes one aficionado. "We could buy the best laundry detergent and it wouldn't break us. We could eat gourmet meals every night and our budget could handle it. We could just buy our kids new stuffed animals instead of making them. But we take a lot of pleasure out of frugal choices and frugal projects in our life."

A Lakewood mother of three, Rena Kellner* echoes these sentiments. She and her husband grew up in financially comfortable homes where they never felt the pinch. As their family grew, however, and resources dwindled, reality hit hard.

"At first, the downsizing and lowering of our *hasagos* was extremely difficult," she admits candidly. "But after a while, we got used to the new routines and even started liking some."

Which brings us to the most common, irrefutable rationale for downsizing: not enough cash. Instead of ending the month in the red, many money-strapped families choose to take charge of their financial destiny by downgrading — in a variety of ways. The results? Hundreds more dollars left in their pockets — or the serenity of soul that comes with staying clear of debt.

WHERE DO YOU START?

Okay, you're convinced. An inspiration to part with possessions wells within, but how to go about it?

It's a big one, but if you have the courage, you can join the millions of people who've chosen to downsize their homes. Once almost exclusively associated with empty-nesters and retirees looking for smaller spaces after the kids have moved out, this move is gaining popularity with a growing number of middle-aged, money-smart homeowners.

"It just made sense for us at this point in our lives," says Canada–based Sari Coffman,* who moved with her husband of 35 years and youngest daughter from a spacious home to a rental duplex. "Owning the house was silly; even when all my marrieds came for Yom Tov the house was too small, and it was too big for us the rest of the year."

The Coffmans have seen firsthand the manifold cost-cutting benefits of home downsizing. For one, they save thousands of dollars each year in mortgage payments — generally the single largest expense consumers face — plus, they're freed from exorbitant property taxes — the next greatest homeowner's outlay.

A smaller place also means fewer dollars spent on utilities.

"Why am I paying to heat and cool an entire basement I never use?" wondered Brooklyn homeowner Risa Thaler* before opting to downsize.

What's more, home downsizing can cut household maintenance in half. Living in a condo, for example, means not having to mow your lawn each week. Fewer bedrooms to paint, for another, means painting job prices drop significantly.

Malka Forster* of Jerusalem remembers a humorous exchange she had with a neighbor shortly after her marriage. On hearing that Malka's apartment had four bedrooms, the *sabra* mother of seven exclaimed, "Why would you want that? It's *so* much to clean!"

"I struggled to keep a straight face," recalls Malka. "I thought, *Is this woman for real? Do I want to move into the likes of her tiny, two-bedroom*

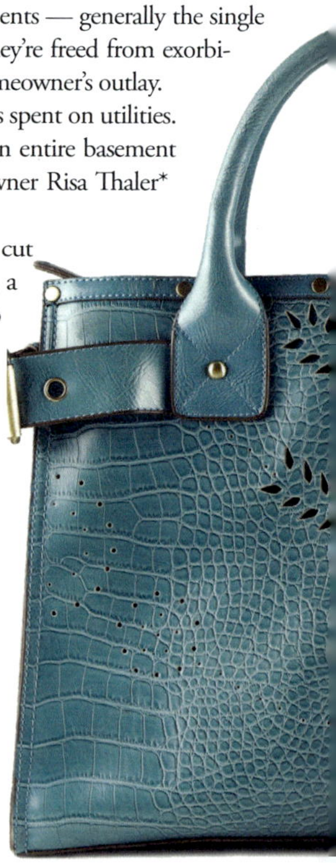

"An abundant life can be spent *doing* things instead of *acquiring* things"

DOWNSIZING: THE PATH TO SPIRITUAL GREATNESS?

Questions and Answers with Rebbetzin Tziporah Heller

If a *frum* Jew was asked, "Does the Torah view downsizing favorably?" he'd probably answer affirmatively. Would you say this is a valid assumption?

It could be, but not necessarily. The Torah views the material world as a means to end; if a person has much – all acquired *b'heter*, all used *l'sheim Shamayim* – there's nothing wrong with that. *Not having* is not a goal. *Having* is not a goal. Using what you have in a way that's appropriate and suits your *avodas Hashem* is the goal.

There have always been people who chose minimal involvement with physical pleasure. A Yerushalmi tzaddik, for example, once tasted an apricot for the first time. He felt such exhilaration that he resolved never to eat an apricot again; the emotional attachment engendered from its taste distracted him from life's real goal.

And it's not just the rich who face the challenge of material attachment: often people with very little are at least as emotionally involved as wealthier individuals, if not more. For example, a minority teenager once killed another teen for his Nike sneakers. Neither teenager had lots of stuff, but clearly, they were deeply attached to "stuff."

Chazal say, "Increase your possessions, and increase your worry." Doesn't that statement clearly support downsizing?

This statement describes a practical reality; it's a nugget of wise advice, not necessarily or exclusively, a directive. The fact is that possessions exact time and space from their owners. The Rambam says that before a person buys something, he should calculate how much it will cost him – not only in money, but in mental energy and maintenance.

Who is a good candidate for downsizing?

Anyone who feels they've become emotionally involved with their things. And taking pride in *not* having – a growing trend in some circles – can also be a form of emotional involvement. Ideally, people should be too busy doing meaningful things with their lives to have time to dwell on assets – whether it's buying more of them or thinking about how few they have.

The *Yated* newspaper once ran a raffle in which every subscriber had a chance to win a variety of prizes. The sweepstakes was entirely computerized, a fact that yielded laughable results: The winner of a set of turquoise towels, as published in the paper, was a "Y.S. Elyashiv" from Yerushalayim. Now, try to envision Rav Elyashiv's *shlita* reaction upon hearing this news. Certainly he didn't say, "That's wonderful! Turquoise towels!" But the *posek hador's* likely indifferent response was not because turquoise towels aren't beautiful or wouldn't enhance his home; it's because he's occupied day and night with things far more eternal than turquoise towels.

An internationally renowned lecturer and author, Rebbetzin Heller's newest project is "Duties of the Heart," an online daily learning program of Chovos HaLevavos.

apartment because it means less sponja?"

Life, however, taught Malka some surprising things.

"As my family grew, and frequent, exhausting cleaning runs became a requisite part of my daily routine, I was finally able to hear her point," she concedes. "I'm not ready to downsize — my place is not that big, after all — but still, I've discovered the kernel of truth in her words."

So how *do* you know if your house is too big for you? One downsizer offers an ingenious gauge: "When two of your bathrooms are regularly dusted rather than cleaned because of non-use!"

For many homeowners, though, the thought of abandoning a house full of wonderful memories and uprooting to an entirely new locale is terrifying. How do downsizers overcome this hurdle?

"I took the most sentimental items with me," says Risa Thaler, whose home of 30 years was actually razed after she sold it, to make room for an all-new mansion. "But more importantly, I moved only a few blocks away. I live in the same community, daven in the same shul, and socialize with the same acquaintances. Now that I've moved, these long-time anchors in my life are what evoke the memories I treasure."

A widow for over a decade now, Risa points out another significant factor: she *chose* to downsize, wanting the security of living near others in an apartment building.

"Because the move was *my* initiative, the transition was easier. I knew this was best for me."

For Sari Coffman, moving into her three-bedroom rental was practically painless because she never developed an attachment to a particular home.

"Over my 35 years of marriage, I moved about ten times," she explains. "And by nature, I'm not an accumulator. When we relocated to Canada from Eretz Yisrael, I left almost everything there. It's not like I own a cherished 25-year-old crib that cradled all six of my children."

But even if she *had* lived in one home for many years, Sari believes she would've downsized anyway, if that's what made sense for her family. The insight Rav Pam *ztz"l* once gave her on a person's ideal relationship to his earthly abode still rings in her ears.

"We once hosted a dinner in our home that Rav Pam attended," recounts Sari. "At that point, we'd finally settled in Canada after fifteen years of marriage — and then my husband felt we should pick up and go to Eretz Yisrael. I was devastated; I'd been so thrilled to have established ourselves in a community.

"I turned to Rav Pam for an *eitzah*. 'This is so hard for me! What should we do?' I cried. Rav Pam listened to the reasoning on both sides and then looked me in the eye. 'Mrs. Coffman,' he said, 'a woman has to be happy with her husband and her children. If you have that, you can move anywhere.' "

JETTISON YOUR JUNK

Some readers will smile in satisfaction (or self-pity!) as they read this article. "Not for me," they think wryly. "I'm downsized to the last penny!" But whatever your financial state, there's the universally applicable, most basic form of downsizing: decluttering.

"Mess brings stress," asserts Yvonne Trostli, a psychotherapist who specializes in chronic disorganization. "You can't see the things that bring you delight because you have too many things to look at."

"We keep things because they're valuable," agrees aspiring downsizer Edna Deblinger, "but if you have to build a new closet or storage room for them, they lose their value."

How to decide what's tossed and what's treasured? According to Barry Izsak, president of the National Association of Professional Organizers and a certified senior move manager in Austin, Texas, anything worth keeping must meet one of the following three criteria: (a) it must be useful and used often; (b) it must be sentimental and extremely rare and special (if you have several such items from one person, you may want to let some go); or (c) it must add to the beauty of your home.

Transplanted New Yorker Shoshana Balaban says she's learned the art of decluttering from her Israeli neighbors, who are pros at living in smaller spaces.

"Before bringing an item into the house, my friends look at it with beady, critical eyes: 'Do we really need it? Where will it go?' For every item they take inside, two items are shipped out."

SIMPLIFYING: IT'S NOT ALWAYS SIMPLE

Despite its numerous benefits, however, no one claims that downsizing is painless. Particularly in today's consumerist climate, where we've been indoctrinated practically since birth to believe that we "need" an untold number of items to attain happiness, it's not easy to go against the tide.

Even psychotherapist Yvonne Trostli admits to a personal struggle. "One part of me that would love to live ...with sparse aesthetics is constantly squabbling with the part that loves the feeling of plenty that comes with a stocked refrigerator and ... a room surrounded by books and sacred objects all in full view."

It's normal to feel this paradox, says Ms. Trostli. But the more you practice letting go, the more familiar — and desirable — the terrain becomes.

"We haven't downsized, we've upsized," affirms Shoshana Balaban, who gave up a well-paying position and American-style home to live in Eretz Yisrael. "Letting go of the extra bandwidth required to maintain our possessions and lifestyle has enormously improved our quality of life."

Shoshana offers as an example the property the Balabans owned in the States. "I had dreams of a magnificent garden, but the land lay bare. I was working full-time and my husband learning; we didn't have the time or resources to tend to it."

Shoshana's current home, by contrast, is bordered by a modest balcony overlooking the verdant Judean Hills.

"It's got a few beautiful plants that we can realistically care for, and I'm thrilled," says Shoshana. "This garden is a fraction of the size, but it's so much more satisfying."

New York Times columnist David Brooks seems to agree, offering a slightly different take on the issue. During his family vacation to the Serengeti, he describes how the more luxurious lodging camps — with showers and pools — felt distinctly colder, while the simpler camps — some without electricity and running water — were warm and cozy.

"It occurred to me that when we moved from a simple camp to a more luxurious camp, we crossed an invisible Heimish Line," he writes.

This phenomenon applies to all aspects of life. Often, contends Mr. Brooks, spending more doesn't mean enjoying more.

"When we're shopping for a vacation we're primarily thinking about *Where* ... But when you come back from vacation, you primarily treasure the memories of *Who* — the people you met from faraway places, and the lives you came in contact with."

Yet another truth corroborating what's consistently emerged from years of happiness research: Better to buy *experiences* than *things*. In other words, memories of a well-planned but not-necessarily-costly Chol HaMoed family trip will be treasured long after the glamour of a new, stylish Yom Tov outfit fades away.

So as we step through the doorways of our succahs this year, leaving behind the creature comforts of our spacious, elegant homes, let's embrace the clarity of soul that comes with living a far more unadorned existence.

Shoshana sums it up as the gift of simplicity. "I have less stuff," she says, "but my life is richer." ■

The following material has been excerpted, with permission, from a series in ***Binah magazine*** *by* ***Shoshana Bernstein*** *entitled:*

A Balancing Act

Real families: Real facts, figures, fears and faith.

Stage 1: Newlyweds

The following interviews reflect the financial reality of two different newlywed couples in Lakewood, New Jersey. For obvious reasons, names have been changed.

Reuven and Cipi Weiss*

Profile

Age: Late twenties
Years married: 2
Children: 1 *ka"h*
Occupation: Wife: *Sheitel macher*
Husband: Start-up company

Financial arrangement

Semi-support
"Our parents generously help with rent and utilities, much to our chagrin. (We wish they didn't have to at all.)"

Monthly salary

Wife:	$3,000

"My husband has begun to set up a start-up company which will hopefully bring in more."

Monthly expenses

Rent:	$900
Utilities:	$300
Total covered by parents:	$1,200
Health Insurance: (plus co-pays)	$1,000
Groceries: (when staying home for Shabbos it can be more)	$700
Taxes:	$600
Car Insurance:	$135
Gas:	$120
Phone/Communications: (necessary for work)	$100
Total:	**$2,655**

Miscellaneous

"We've been paying $350 a month to pay off the deductibles from our baby's birth. We made our final payment this month! Hooray! "Plus, every so often we go clothes- shopping, buy 'treats' and flowers for Shabbos, and gifts. Car repairs cost money, and we are working on paying off our debt."

Debt

Credit card: (approximately)	$3,500

"We're actively working on it — it was accrued through unexpected emergency circumstances at the start of our marriage."

Savings

$20,000-30,000

Chasunah money, some money from before marriage
$3,000 – Gift money for the child in her own account
"We try to put aside between $50 and $100 each month, no matter what."

Additional pertinent information

"Summer work will hopefully pay off another chunk of debt… we both freelance too, trying to work it off. But no matter how much 'extra' there seems to be, it doesn't last longer than butter in a hot pan…"

Can you describe the financial arrangements that you have?

Cipi: I work full-time from home, which on a good week means about 30 hours a week, Sunday through Friday. We receive $1,200 in support to cover our rent and utilities.

We're not eligible for government aid. My friend works fewer hours, makes less money, and gets free health insurance. That's at least $12,000 I'm spending out of pocket (and let's not even *start* talking about co-pays, deductibles, or dental, which I just don't have at this point because it's so pricey.)

What has been the most difficult aspect of having to transition from being a single twenty-four-year-old with minimal expenses to a married woman with financial responsibilities?

So many *expenses*! I mean, rent alone is insane! Money goes like water before you're even spending on things you *want* to spend on. I never had that before.

Do you factor "me" money into your budget? What about birthday presents and Chanukah gifts?

I love giving gifts. It's my thing. But I try to be smart about it, going for the "shtick" factor rather than the "expensive" bit. I'll shop around or buy in the dollar store and write an adorable note, packaging the whole thing beautifully. (I keep ribbons when I get gifts, so I'm never short.) I'll also bake something if I have time – it's the thought that counts. But yeah, it ends up costing.

How does the reality of being supported measure up with your expectations?

I dreaded being supported. I hate knowing that my hardworking parents and in-laws are pressured to give me anything. I wish I could give *them*! I dream of the day when *iy"H* we'll be able to support ourselves without having to give them extra things to worry about – they give us so much already! My biggest dream? Making enough money to pay them back, so that they can relax a little, maybe even use it to support other siblings or things like that. I really wish I didn't have to take any money from them, but if I didn't, I'd be out on the street. And I can't work any harder or make any more money at this point.

Can you share a couple of examples of specific financial difficulties that have arisen in the past few months?

Yeah. The car's "cluster" broke. Whatever that is. Now we're a couple of hundred smackers poorer and the CD player *still* doesn't work.

Insurance is insane. I picked the most expensive plan we can (barely) afford, asked all the right questions, and still got nailed with a $1,000 fee for a service I thought was covered. I broke down in tears on the phone with the representative and now I am *davening* that my appeal letter, er, *appeals* to their more gracious side. We shall see.

If you could have any one question answered regarding your finances, what would it be?

How is this supposed to work?! Seriously! And how does *anyone* do it when they have to pay tuition? Maybe I should homeschool my kids when they get old enough… or win the lottery. How do people afford normal health insurance?

Shimon and Rochel Hirsch*

Profile

Age: Twenties
Years married: 4
Children: 3 *ka"h*
Occupation: Wife: Speech language pathologist
Husband: Learning full-time

Financial arrangement

No support

Monthly salary

Wife:	$3,000
Husband: Night *seder*	$150

Monthly expenses

Rent and utilities:	$900
Groceries:	$500
Daycare:	$545
Student loan:	$250
Car Insurance:	$100
Gas:	$300
Phone:	$83
Total:	**$2,678**

Debt

Student loans:	$15,000

"We have a credit card which we use to accrue miles. When we do use a credit card, it's instead of cash and we pay it off."

Savings

$5,000

Additional pertinent details

"I'm a speech language pathologist with a Masters in science. I was recently laid off due to budget cuts. I have been sending out my résumé to try to find a new job. I'm hoping to get unemployment benefits and find a tutoring job for the summer."

As a young girl growing up and nearing marriageable age, did you imagine that this would be the kind of life you would lead?

Rochel: My greatest desire was to have a husband who would learn long-term. My father works now, but he started his married life learning, and we were raised with *yeshivishe hashkafos* and true Torah values. My father learns whenever he has a free minute, and my mother instilled in us the beauty of a Torah home and a desire to marry someone who learns.

How do your expectations match up with the reality of having no one to depend on for financial assistance?

I don't think I realized how hard it would be. I never knew how much it costs just to live. In putting together the numbers for this article, I couldn't believe how much it was! Truthfully, I was under the impression that I would be supported for longer. I thought that I would be able to buy a home just like everyone else. My parents offered to pay for my undergrad schooling or for a house, and I chose education, and now it will be many years until I can own a home.

For the first two years, I did have some financial assistance with paying my rent – I was not working and was in school full-time, and had no income at all. Our *chasunah* money was used to pay for food and gas expenses.

You are basically the sole provider for your family. How do you feel about being the one who is working so hard to meet your family's financial needs?

I'm your regular, typical "with it" girl. I daven that Hashem should give me *kochos* to be able to do this as long as possible. Each and every day I wake up at 6:30 a.m. so I can be ready to leave the house at 7:30. I say to myself: "Hashem, please give me the strength to be able to make it through the day. I am only doing this so that my husband can sit and learn." I am happy and willing to work so that my husband can sit and learn.

I thank Hashem that I was fortunate enough to have a good job this year and daven that I should be able to find a job that's equally good or better for next year (since I was laid off).

What are some of the challenges you face, living in a community where so many other couples are receiving at least some help from their parents?

It is very challenging. Just a couple of days ago, I was outside talking to a neighbor of mine. We were discussing the pros and cons of working, and she told me that she will be working only part-time next year, since it got too difficult for her. She feels she just needs to be home with her children, and *parnassah* is in the hands of Hashem, and He sends what you need. I don't think she appreciates or even realizes that not everyone is being helped financially. She can afford to work part-time, because she has parental support.

Can you share an example of a specific money-related difficulty that has arisen in the past few months?

I love my daughter's teacher, and I really wanted to buy her an end-of-the-year present. I felt it was important that she receive a gift to show how much I appreciate and value all she's done for my child. But I just didn't have the budget to cover something expensive. It turns out that this same teacher will be with my daughter in day camp, so I plan to make her an ice cream pie. *Baruch Hashem*, I have the knack for creativity, so instead of spending money, I'll do something creative. It's not an expensive gift, but it will nonetheless show my appreciation.

Are there any suggestions or tips that you wish someone would have told you, which you can offer others who find themselves in a similar financial situation?

Yes!

Firstly, I see people shopping for groceries, and they just take anything off the shelves. When you go shopping, look at the prices! That one minute of looking can save you many minutes of working. The same item can vary in price by a dollar or more, depending on the company. Beware of stores that don't post their prices on the shelves. Get into the habit of pricing basics that you use often, such as diapers. Call the stores that sell the item you want, and find out who's cheaper. When an item goes on sale, like cereal, tissues, cups, aluminum pans, I try to stock up. It saves me so much money.

Recently, I had a conversation with my mother about my sisters and seminary. I suggested that maybe she should give my sisters the option to choose either seminary or a down payment for a house. I don't know what I would have chosen at the time, but in hindsight I now know how hard it is and hope my sisters will have an easier time. In fact, one sister is getting married soon, and I told her she's lucky to be single and be in college. By getting married later, she has been able to go to school, work, and pay off her student loans. The same loans that I took with me into my marriage, she will have paid off before she gets married. Not that I regret marrying when I did, but I was at least able to offer her a different perspective and show her how grateful she can be.

Stage 2: The Growing Family

The following two mothers have taken time from their very busy days to give us a glimpse into their financial life and show us what works, what doesn't, and how they feel about it all.

Motty & Elisheva Gross*

Profile

Age: 35 and 38
Years married: 15
Children: 5, ranging in age from 2 to 12 years
Occupation: Husband: Special-education tutor, full day
Wife: Part-time office manager

Financial arrangement

No support

Monthly salary

Husband: (fluctuates)	$5,500
Wife:	$2,500
Total:	**$8,000**

Monthly expenses

Rent:	$2,000
Food:	$1,400
Tuition:	$1,330
Daycare:	$1,110
Insurance for wife:	$480
Car insurance:	$378
Car lease:	$290
Electric:	$210
Bus:	$125
Insurance for children: (CHP)	$90
Phone/Communications:	$90
Cell phones:	$80
Gas:	$45
Child with specialized needs — tutoring and lessons:	$1,200
Total:	**$8,618**
Total Annual Expenses:	**$103,416**
Total income:	**$96,000**

Debt

Friend:	$17,500
Family:	$4,000
Small loan:	$275

My husband worked as a *rebbi* for years before making a career switch this year to a government job where the pay comes on time. The yeshivah still owes him $35,000 dollars for last year! Our debt was accrued over time when there was nothing to live off. We didn't live beyond our means, but it did add up and we were forced to borrow. We have no credit card bills other than monthly, which we always pay up in full.

Savings

None. All depleted due to a medical crisis. We hope that the $50,000 we laid out will come back one day. If it does, it will be divided to begin saving for our children's weddings.

When did your husband stop learning full time? Was that a difficult decision?

Elisheva: My husband was learning full time for the first four years of our marriage. It was a torturous decision for both of us when he switched to learning half a day, but the reality was we could not make it work anymore.

He continued learning in the morning and began teaching English in the afternoons. This brought in a decent income, but the following year when he was offered a full day teaching job he couldn't turn it down. I am grateful for the years he was able to learn, but I was getting exhausted from being the sole breadwinner and I think my husband saw that. He always said, "I appreciate what you do and I want to continue learning forever, but it's my *kesubah,* not yours... Let me know if it gets too hard."

As your children grew and started school, how did you incorporate tuition into your budget?

When our tuition obligations started, my husband and I sat down and made two crucial decisions:

1: We will *im yirtzeh Hashem* always pay tuition the way we pay rent — the first of the month, no matter what. As people who have been involved in the *chinuch* world, we've seen the devastating effects of parents not paying tuition. It's a ripple effect: I'm owed money, therefore I owe my grocer, and then he can't pay his child's tuition, and the *Rebbi* and teachers suffer even more.

2: For the *chinuch* of our children, there are no compromises. Money can't and won't be an issue if a child needs tutoring or mentoring. We don't ask for a tuition discount. I would be embarrassed to ask my grocer for a discount on eggs — I trust that his price is fair. Same with tuition.

Of all the expenses you face, which do you find most stressful?

My credit card bill! Over the course of the month I charge all utility, tuition and food bills, and then I wait for the money, which is rightfully mine, to come in. When it doesn't, I go nuts, but *baruch Hashem* we usually pull through. We've had to borrow from time to time, which is horrible. I hate debt. I also worry about how we'll manage in general when I look at our budget and see that on paper we shouldn't be making it.

Who is in charge of paying the bills?

Ahhhh. In the beginning, it was me, but when the stress began killing me, my husband took over. I went bonkers! He bounced checks and did a messy job, but he got it done, whereas I could not. Now we divide it 50/50. I take care of actually paying the bills, but I often warn him about a bill coming due and that I need the money to somehow appear....

Do you have a weekly or monthly budget?

I've given up on budgeting for a while. I hope that as soon as my husband's job begins in September, we'll go back to it. The way I work things is that my salary check gets put into an envelope and I don't deposit it right away — I save it to pay for my insurance and rent. This way, I know I have the money set aside for both, and it isn't being spent on anything else. I deposit the check on the 28th of the month and make out the rent and insurance check right way for the first of the month. I'd love to do that with all our money: divide it into envelopes and only spend what's inside. But that would only work when I actually have the money!

Can you share your strategies for coping with financial stress?

My husband says: Pray, pray and pray. Oh, and then be proactive and take on whatever menial job is offered that will help keep us going. And then keep counting your blessings.

As for me, I spend! Seriously, when I know I'm in the throes of a debt crisis, I cope by spending. It's dangerous, and not something I encourage, but those are the moments when I finally have the urge to spend, no matter what the amount. I've gotten to know that dark side of me and have worked on it — mainly by pushing off the purchase until I'm reasonable enough to understand that this is not what I really want. I really don't want to be poorer!

If you could have any question answered regarding your finances, what would it be?

Since I can't lower my expenses significantly enough for it to make a difference, what can I do to raise my income? How can I cut food expenses?

Nechemia & Shira Dubovsky*

Profile

Age: [illegible]
Years married: 11
Children: 6 ranging from newborn to age 10
Occupation: Husband: CPA full time
Wife: formerly a secretary in a doctor's office, and now home full time.

Monthly salaries:

From husband's job	$10,600
Income from rent of small apartment we have downstairs	$1,300
Total:	**$ 11,900**

Monthly expenses:

Expense	**Amount**
Mortgage	$3,200
Home Insurance	$250
Auto insurance	$310
Health Insurance Plan $1,300 + $400 in copays =	$1,700
Food/staple groceries	$1,700
Take out	$100
Phone:	$40
Gas:	$75
Electricity:	$200
Cell phone for my husband:	$59
Monthly for gas and car wash	$400
Tuition 5 children	$2,300
Building funds combined:	$1,000
Taxes:	$100
Cleaning Help:	$250
Clothing:	

I estimate that I spend about $2,800 annually on the kids combined, $1,000 on myself, and $500 on my husband.

Total Monthly Expenses:	**$11,747.50**
Total Annual Expenses:	**$140,970**
Total income:	**$142,800**

Debt:

None. Whatever we put on the credit card is paid by the end of the month. My in-laws live a frugal lifestyle and were able to pay for my husband's education. They also helped us with rent and other basic expenses while he went to school. It prevented us from falling into debt like others that I know did.

Savings: $6,000

We depleted our savings when we bought our house, but for the last year or so I've managed to put away $500 monthly — not a lot, and I'd like to put away more, but it's a start. We're saving towards bar mitzvahs and *chasunos*, and eventually we'd like to put away some money so we can go on vacation every once in a while. So far, that's a luxury I can't afford. I also would love to have a retirement fund.

Your husband is an accountant. Did you always plan on marrying a working boy? Was he working when you got married or was he still in school?

Shira: My parents are both hard working people, and all my siblings married long time learning boys. I, on the other hand, always enjoyed shopping and having nice things, and I knew and my parents knew that I was not cut out for that kind of life. My parents taught me about spending responsibly, and that you don't ever spend more than you earn. And I knew I wanted to spend. So... where did that leave me?! I knew I had to marry someone who would earn a living.

My husband was learning when we got married, which was important to me because I wanted someone who was in a Torah environment. However, we were both honest about our future plans and I knew that he was planning to get a degree a year or so later.

I was plotzing for him to start working so I could start spending, and you know what? I needed to learn *fast* that if I didn't curb my desires, if I didn't stop swiping that plastic — we wouldn't have a penny for food or rent. My husband knew from the start that I am more of a spender, but I don't think he foresaw how much it would affect him.

So, I canceled the internet in my home so I couldn't do online shopping at the drop of a hat, and I began learning a *mussar* sefer with my husband to keep me in check. It helped to realize that it was hurting my husband when I spent his hard-earned money in seconds, money that took hours and hours for him to make.

As your children grew up and started school, how did you incorporate tuition into your budget?

Baruch Hashem, that was just when my husband got a raise, and we both said: "Tuition!"

Do you have a weekly budget? How do you incorporate the costs of Yomim Tovim and summertime into your expenses?

I have a monthly budget that covers the recurring expenses. I have an annual budget that I try not to exceed for expenses like clothing and Yom Tov costs. I deduct that money every week so that when I need more before Yom Tov, it's okay, and then for the next couple of months I know I need to lay low. In fact, we keep spreadsheets of all our expenses and compare them after Yom Tov is over to see how we can do better next time and why.

If you could have a question answered regarding your finances, what would it be?

1: How do you stop yourself from spending when you see a "good buy"? I can't seem to hold back when I see a great bargain, and the small things add up.

2: Is there a work-from-home job, not too many hours, that is lucrative? I would like to do something in the evenings for a few hours and have money to put away.

Your financial profile seems to present a rosier picture than others we have interviewed. Do you have financial stress in your life?

Since my husband is a CPA, I have a different kind of stress. In general, he works a 45-hour work week, 8 a.m.-6 p.m. Monday through Thursday, and 9 a.m.-2 p.m. on Friday. He comes home during my wackiest hour and he leaves during the time I need help most. Erev Pesach is my husband's craziest season, and I don't get any help at all from him. Sometimes I resent his being busy but then I remind myself that I'm the one who wants this lifestyle and I can't have it both ways.

I know that some people reading this may say, "What stress?! She's paying her bills, her husband makes a good living, and she's not working." I really agreed to this interview so that I could enlighten others. The assumption that someone like me does not have financial stress is both unfair and incorrect. I know that people look at me and say I totally can't relate to economic difficulties, but that's just not true. People need to understand that everyone has to live within her means, and for every person that presents her own, very real challenge. Less immediate, perhaps, but the stress and the challenge are there nonetheless.

Mesila Education Division

CORE VALUES AND CONCEPTS

A Believing Jew's Attitude Towards Finance

- **Bitachon:** Believing that Hashem gives every person exactly what he needs, for his benefit.
- **Halachah:** A Jew cannot expect to be financially stable unless he follows halachos of money to the letter.
- **Responsibility:** Realizing that the Torah obligates us to take reasonable measures to protect our own and others' money and belongings.
- **Contentment:** Being satisfied with what we have.

Financial Management

- **Awareness and control:** Keeping track of what we have and what we spend enables us to make sensible decisions.
- **Planning ahead:** If you fail to plan, you plan to fail.
- **Paying attention to details:** Little things add up very quickly; attention to detail can make the difference between success and failure.
- **Resourcefulness:** Learning to work creatively with what we have and making it work for us.

Responsibility to Others

- **Integrity:** Honesty in money matters and in all areas, big and small.
- **Respecting property:** Accepting boundaries and respecting the property of others, as well as our own.
- ***Chessed* and *tzedakah*:** Appreciating that our money is entrusted to us to share with others.

Peer Pressure

- **Positive peer pressure:** Recognizing that our actions impact what others will do and using that realization to trigger positive change.
- **Negative peer pressure:** Resisting blindly following friends' example and currying their approval, when it can be detrimental.
- **Critical social observation:** Learning to resist advertising lures, subtle or overt.

Communication

- **Relationships:** Healthy communication - respectfully and effectively expressing our needs regarding money - is key to healthy relationships especially with our parents.
- **Maturity:** Calm and focused communication regarding money promotes a more mature thought process and helps curtail feelings of entitlement.

Money and Materialism

- **Money is a means only:** Material gain is not an end in itself, but rather a tool to enable the effective implementation of Torah values.
- **Defining satisfaction:** Learning to identify satisfaction with values, relationships, and accomplishments, irrelevant of size of bank account.
- **Resisting materialism:** Withstanding the excessive emphasis on material goods.
- **Delayed gratification:** Waiting for things we really want brings emotional and material dividends.
- **Thinking independently:** What others have or need is not necessarily what we have or need – avoiding comparisons.

Prioritizing

- **Needs and wants:** Differentiating between needs and wants: Needs become stronger with time, while wants wane.
- **Balancing needs and wants:** Defining the financial goal as ensuring that we have everything we need and some of what we want.
- **Importance of prioritizing:** Ranking demands and desires and balancing time, energy, and money according to thought-out priorities.

Made in the USA
Las Vegas, NV
03 November 2026

57421602R00093